DAVID
CAMPESE

A Ernie & Pat

the best thing come from

down under

da

[signature]

DAVID CAMPESE

Co-ordinated by David Clark

IRONBARK LEGENDS

IRONBARK
Pan Macmillan Australia

First published 1996 in Ironbark by Pan Macmillan Australia Pty Limited
St Martins Tower, 31 Market Street, Sydney

National Library of Australia
cataloguing-in-publication data:

David Campese
ISBN 0 7329 0850 7
1. Campese, David. 2. Rugby Union football players –
Australia – Biography. (Series: Ironbark legends).
796.333092

Designed by Mark Thacker, Big Cat Design
Printed in Australia by McPherson's Printing Group

Dedicated to those who not
only enjoy rugby, but believe in it.
Thank you for supporting me.

ACKNOWLEDGEMENTS

Thanks to Trevor McKewan, Doug Golightly, Ray Cairns, John Griffiths, Liz Herbert, Greg Thomas, ACT Rugby, Russell Vine, and the State Library of NSW.
In particular I would like to thank Philip Derriman and all my sponsors.

CONTENTS

David Ian Campese
CAREER MILESTONES

Born 21 October, 1962, Queanbeyan, NSW to Gianantonio and Joan Campese. Brother Mario (born 1959) , sisters Lisa (1964) and Corrina (1965).

Campese family moves back to Montecchio Precalcino in northern Italy in 1966 for eighteen months and returns to Australia and settles again in Queanbeyan the following year.

Attends local public school and high school. Plays rugby league from the ages of eight to sixteen for the Queanbeyan Blues.

Wins the ACT-Monaro Schoolboys golf title in 1978.

First game of rugby union for the Queanbeyan Whites club in the ACT rugby competition in 1979 in fourth grade. Promoted to first grade in 1980.

Selected for the Australian Under 21 side against New Zealand, Sydney Cricket Ground, 1982, at the age of nineteen.

Selected on the 1982 Wallaby tour of New Zealand after ten established Australian players withdraw. Makes his Test debut for Australia at Lancaster Park in Christchurch on 14 August and scores one try.

Scores four tries in Australia's first official Test match v USA in July, 1983 at the Sydney Cricket Ground, equalling Greg Cornelsen's record for the most tries in a Test by an Australian.

Member of the 1984 Wallaby Tour of Great Britain that won rugby's 'grand slam', the first Australian side to defeat all four home sides, England, Ireland, Wales and Scotland, on a tour.

Plays for Italian club Petrarca in the northern city of Padua from 1984–88 during the northern winter. Transfers to the Amatori club in Milan in 1988, owned by Italian media magnate and future Prime Minister Silvio Berlusconi, and plays with them until 1993.

Member of the 1986 side that beat the All Blacks 2–1 in New Zealand, only the fourth international and the second Australian team to win a Test series in New Zealand.

1987–joins Sydney club Randwick from the Queanbeyan Whites.

Receives a standing ovation from the crowd and applause from his teammates after scoring a zig-zagging try for Australia against the Barbarians at Cardiff Arms Park in 1988. Campese regards this as his best try in international rugby.

July 1989–a misguided pass behind the line directed at Greg Martin allows Ieuan Evans to score and the British Lions to win the series, the low point of his career on the field.

Plays his fiftieth Test match for Australia v France in Sydney, June, 1990.

July 1990–misses selection from the Australian team to play France following his late return from Italy.

October/November 1991–acclaimed the Player of the 1991 World Cup, scoring six tries in as many matches for the victorious Wallabies. The second pool match against Western Samoa is Campese's sixtieth Test, breaking the record for the most number of Test appearances for Australia. The final against England at Twickenham is Campese's 100th international match for Australia.

August 1992–scores his fiftieth Test try in Cape Town, in the first Test match between Australia and South Africa since 1971.

September 1992–opens Campo's Sport and Leisure store at St Ives shopping centre in Sydney with business partner Julie McGraw.

Member of Australia's third World Cup squad in South Africa. Defending champions Australia bow out in the quarter-finals against England.

Omitted from the side to play the first Test v New Zealand in Auckland in the 1995 Bledisloe Cup series. He is a late selection onto the bench in the second Test in Sydney, then runs on as a replacement to notch up his ninety-second Test cap.

June 1996–second Test v Wales in Sydney is Campese's ninety-fourth—second on the all-time list of Test appearances for all nations.

Winners take chances

Winners take chances.
Like everyone else they fear failing,
but they refuse to let fear control them.
Winners don't give up.
When life gets tough they hang in
until the going gets better.
Winners are flexible.
They realise there is more than one way
and are willing to try others.
Winners know they are not perfect.
They respect their weaknesses
while making the most of their strengths.
Winners fall, but they don't stay down.
They stubbornly refuse to let a fall
keep them from climbing.
Winners don't blame fate for their failures,
nor luck for their successes.
Winners accept responsibility for their lives.
Winners are positive thinkers
who see good in all things.
From the ordinary, they make the extraordinary.
Winners believe in the path they have chosen
even when it's hard
even when others can't see
where they are going.
Winners are patient.
They know a goal is only as worthy as the
effort that's required to achieve it
Winners are people like you.
They make this world a better place.

Nancye Sims

FOREWORD

I t is a great pleasure to be involved in a publication that will be the first edition of a series dedicated to great Australian sports men and women. David Campese is widely regarded as the greatest rugby player of his generation. In *David Campese*, ten commentators, including rugby writers, friends, fellow players and opponents on the field have all come together to give an insight into this great player. The book is richly illustrated with over 100 photographs, many of them never published before.

David Campese first made the Australian rugby fraternity stand up and take notice when he played fullback for the Australian Capital Territory Under 21 team in an early fixture to an international at the Sydney Cricket Ground in July, 1982. He continuously brought the massive crowd to its feet with his unorthodox style and free running. From that day, David Campese stamped his mark on the game and within weeks he had been elevated to the Australian team.

His unique style has influenced many players. I recall a story that whilst he was playing in Italy, he took the field with his wrists taped and a week later every player in Italy had his wrists taped the same way! This is the magnetism of the man. He has left his mark off the field as well; his constructive criticism of rugby officials, including coaches, has been forthright, often controversial and at times rather refreshing.

Rugby was established on mateship, a game one plays to enjoy. Although rugby has only recently turned professional at the elite level, David's style and approach to the game has always been that way. His dedication and preparation for any match should be a model to all young, aspiring players. The likes of David Campese don't surface often—he is a credit to the game both on and off the field.

My previous record for the number of Test matches played by an Australian (thirty) over a period of eleven years looks miniscule against David's ninety-odd tests in an international career spanning fourteen years. He enjoys the game so much, I'm sure he could go on playing forever if he wanted.

Nicholas Shehadie
Sir Nicholas Shehadie AC, OBE

THE CROOKED ROAD TO GENIUS

by Gordon Bray

No-one has spoken more words about David Campese than television commentator Gordon Bray, who has called nearly every Test match he has played. Here he gives an insight into Campese the man, on and off the field.

Campo hoists one high for Randwick.

The reception couldn't
have been warmer when
Australia's victorious
World Cup team came
home to a Sydney
4   ticker-tape parade in 1991.

Campo is like your favourite LP record. His illustrious career has reached its twilight and although the reproduction may have become a bit crackly, the essential quality endures. On any rugby pitch he has always enjoyed being the centre of attention. As long as that athletic, fast-twitching frame can continue to react so intuitively, there will be plenty more worthwhile encores to enjoy.

But...there does come a time.

Beneath the public exterior of David Ian Campese lies a complex character. A loner, an extremely sensitive person, but also a supreme opportunist. His commercial successes have been well documented. After the 1991 World Cup, it was rumoured that Network Ten signed him up for three years on a six-figure annual sum, just for promotions. At the time, no rugby player past or present could claim that level of financial backing from television.

Campo is always his own man and if you don't like the offerings then that's your problem. Criticism rarely sits well, yet he's not one to harbour grudges. Loyalty is everything. The man has learned to be a survivor and isn't shy to contact his friends in high places. How else (a cynic might ask) did he manage to take the field in the Centenary Bledisloe Cup match against the All Blacks in Sydney, when most rugby critics placed him at no better than third or fourth in line? By all reports, coach Bob Dwyer had made it clear to his most celebrated Wallaby that 'the crooked road' had finally come to a dead end. Perhaps it was divine intervention. And why not? Surely Australian rugby owed him that modest concession. (After all, Campese's 27 Tests against the All Blacks is more than any other player in history.)

At the end of the 1987 season, the Wallabies under Alan Jones had not only 'bombed out' in the World Cup but lost a series in Argentina as well. Campese gave the ARU hierarchy an ultimatum. 'It's Jones or me. He goes or I go.' They may be a conservative bunch at times, but the custodians of Australian rugby know their game and the value of its on-field exponents. Jones departed, Campese stayed, and Bob Dwyer returned as coach. But, eight seasons later, Campese's relationship with the national coach had deteriorated beyond repair. Privately, Campo believed the Wallabies had lost the plot. There were too many 'old men' in the forwards, he reckoned. For Dwyer's part, his star winger had simply lost the old sparkle.

By season's end, all these negatives outweighed the positives and the rift was beginning to harm what had been a magnificent

team spirit. Dwyer went, Campese stayed. The breakdown between these two great free spirits of rugby was a symptom of a deeper malaise that disrupted and ultimately brought down Australia's World Cup campaign.

David Campese likes to play his rugby on the highwire—without a safety net. When he slips, the result can be catastrophic. Thankfully, those moments have been few, and, in overall context, insignificant. Here is a sportsman who translates rare ability into pleasure, for himself and his army of fans. The stumbles are part of the package. Campo is the embodiment of the notion that without risk there can be no adventure. When he pulls on that no.11 rugby jumper the 'comfort zone' becomes instantly derestricted. The same applied to his close mate Mark Ella. They were both instinctive and unpredictable. My greatest regret in rugby is that those two kindred souls didn't play another five seasons or more together in Wallaby colours. Unquestionably, the firm of Campese & Ella brought together two of the greatest broken field runners of all time.

Who can forget Campese's first Test against the All Blacks at Lancaster Park, Christchurch in 1982? A cross-field kick from skipper Ella and suddenly this irreverent teenager from the ACT had left the world's best winger, Stu Wilson, in his wake. Coach Dwyer had backed his judgement by choosing the youngster and in the following Test in Wellington (won 19–16 by Australia) the New Zealand rugby public understood why. The junior maestro handled twice in Gary Ella's try and then finished off one of the most stirring support tries in Test match history. More than half the Wallaby side handled in the movement, starting with Cox and Mark Ella. Then Gould, Grigg, Gary Ella, Hawker, Lucas and big Steve Williams all combined before Campo scooted over beside the posts. It was a knockout blow on half-time and gave the Australians a match-winning 19–3 lead. For any remaining doubters, those tries in each of his first two Tests against the All Blacks were testimony to the arrival of an international rugby star.

But even in those formative years rough water was always close by. In the lead-up match to the third and deciding Test on that '82 tour, the Wallabies just managed to hold out North Auckland at Whangarei by 16–12. Campese notched two tries, a penalty and a conversion, for a thirteen point personal tally. He was duly named 'man of the match'. At the following press conference, however, Dwyer came out with his six-shooter blazing: 'Campese was dreadful. He used his great skills to do some brilliant things, but the rest of the match he just wasted his time. Campese was awful, absolutely bloody awful. He didn't use his head in the entire game and lost the ball in the tackle on every single occasion.'

It could only happen to Campo, and would continue to happen for the next decade or more. Because he carries everyone's highest expectations, frustration soon sets in if he falls short. There would

be more of the same during the following tour of New Zealand in '86 under Jones. After winning the first Test in Wellington, the Wallabies were robbed of a series victory in the second when Welsh referee Derek Bevan disallowed a legitimate try by Steve Tuynman. The enigmatic Jones was Campo's greatest admirer, but after a wretched day at fullback, that relationship soured. 'Today we played without a fullback,' commented Jones to a group of exhausted players in the Australian dressing room.

Later that night in Jones' room, Campo copped another withering tongue-lashing from the coach for his inept performance. So distraught was he in a nightclub a few hours later, that he declared he was ready to retire from rugby. It was distressing to see such a gifted athlete and entertainer so despondent and agitated. The world's rugby enthusiasts can be grateful that Mark Ella consoled his teammate that night. After

(opposite) Is this the famous goose-step caught on celluloid? (above) It's too little too late from England's Chris Oti as a happy Campese touches down. Australia v England, Sydney Football Stadium, 1991.

7

Classic Campo—snapped in full flight as Will
Carling (centre) and Nick Popplewell (right)
lead the chase. Australia v Barbarians, 1992.

(opposite) Putting the boot in for NSW v ACT, Canberra, 1994.
(left) The glittering prize—Campo with the World Cup, Twickenham, November 2, 1991.
(below) AFL clubs eat your hearts out! Campo flies high.

switching back to wing, Campese scored the Bledisloe Cup-clinching try at Eden Park. (His replacement at fullback was Andrew Leeds who made a smashing test debut.)

Campo always seemed to give the impression that he was an easy target—a ready-made scapegoat for coaches when things went wrong because he was never entirely without guilt. That's the nature of his personal and sporting philosophy...sometimes dazzling, sometimes perplexing—and sometimes both of those qualities in the same breath. I have always maintained that Campo's confidence must be carefully protected—'wrapped in cotton wool' if you like. When a player has the ability to perform at another level, then we have to be tolerant. That is especially true when the same individual bruises easily. Encourage rather than criticise.

But Campo's critics will be quick to parry: 'hang on, you're talking about a gun-slinger who shoots off on a wing and a prayer.' Why should we have one set of rules for Campo and another for the rest? The point needs to be met. In a team context, the case for Campo's fading star at national level looks a trifle shaky, especially if all his cylinders aren't firing. But it's also fair to say at state level he's always prospered. Perhaps he feels more comfortable because among the Waratahs he's accepted for who he is and what he stands for, by teammates, coaches and support staff who know him better. I lean towards Aristotle's theory that 'no great genius is without an admixture of madness.' The great Greek philosopher also said that 'all men of genius are naturally melancholic.'

Campese is a perfectionist. He becomes frustrated when he fails to reach his self-imposed high standards on the field. He also lets himself become upset when fellow players aren't tuned-in to his particular vision. But the indisputable bottom line is that he has always remained loyal to the game he loves so passionately.

(below) Campese with fellow Channel Ten commentators Nick Farr-Jones (left) and Gordon Bray (centre).
(opposite) What it's all about—the World Cup (top) and the Bledisloe Cup (below).

My lasting memory of Campo will be his performances in the '91 World Cup where he was acclaimed 'Player of the Tournament'. He mesmerised the Pumas at Llanelli, humbled Wales at the Arms Park and then provided that composed 'flip ball' for Michael Lynagh in those last dramatic moments against Ireland at Lansdowne Road.

His try against the All Blacks in the semi-final was pure vintage Campese. John Kirwan and his teammates tried to second guess Campo's intentions. He kept them guessing all the way to the goal-line. It was a mortal blow for the defending champions. A humiliation from which they never recovered. Then came *that* pass to Tim Horan for the try of the tournament in the same game. With the final still to play, Campo had already proved himself to be the most gifted and entertaining footballer of the era.

International rugby will never again see the likes of David Campese. Forget his faults: here is a rugby man of true distinction—a Ferrari engine in a Rolls-Royce body. My fond hope is that his flame will inspire other young players to always carry the sword to the opposition with excitement and flair. Every team needs a rebel of his ilk, someone to say, 'let's give it a go, and bugger the consequences.'

Thanks Campo.

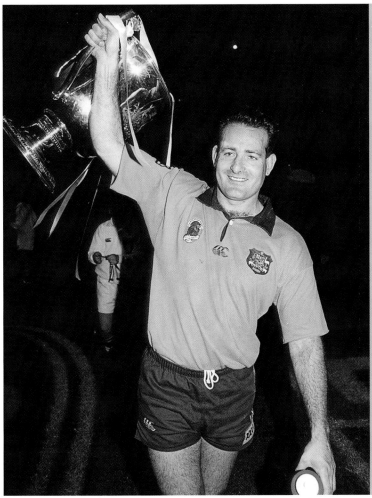

'Like Pele, he is associated with the very best and historic moments in sport; he has a special genius which shows that an individual can still paint his own portrait and leave an indelible mark for all to treasure. The ingredients are the same: stature, presence, personality, style and an immense belief in the God-given talents.'

Barry John,
former Welsh fly half

ONLY CAMPO COULD DO THAT

by Stu Wilson

David Campese has played more Test matches against New Zealand than any other player in history. Former All Black winger Stu Wilson remembers how Campese hit the headlines in New Zealand before he even played his first game...

Campese dives to score the first try of the 1991 World Cup semi-final against New Zealand.

'll never forget David Campese's arrival on the international stage. How could I? Back in 1982 when the Wallabies arrived in New Zealand the brash youngster, who hadn't pulled on the green and gold jersey, was already being heralded as one of the better wingers to have come here. I took it all in my stride, after all I was constantly being written up as being at the top of my game and to be honest I wasn't playing too badly.

But my old mate Bernie Fraser, who hung out on the other wing, believed this bloke was 'special' and had given me a fair ribbing about marking him. 'Let's wait and see if he's up to it,' I told Bernie quietly.

I didn't have to wait long to realise that David was a special breed. He proved that minutes after he arrived at Auckland Airport. When asked by a television reporter if he was looking forward to marking Stu Wilson he replied, 'Stu who?' That one cocky statement set him apart as a player to be both respected and challenged. Here was a bloke who didn't fear anything or anyone. He exuded all the confidence and self-belief that most Australian rugby players have of right, yet there was a wonderful twinkle in his eye.

It was the glint of a rugby rebel in those eyes that made me acutely aware that this was no ordinary player. And David proved

that in '82 and has gone on doing it ever since.

I only got four Tests against him because I pulled the pin on rugby after our crushing series win against the British Lions in 1983 but I can put one hand over the heart, and say, 'There weren't too many better', despite it being the infancy of his career.

I've always regarded him highly, so much so that he was the first player I invited to play in a benefit game a year later! It's a much overused term nowadays but it was his 'vision' that made him stand out. Add to that his slick ball skills, the ability to step off either foot, his acceleration and his anticipation and you had a player of rare class. I know we were always concerned that whenever he got the ball something was always on and he had to be watched. 'What the hell's he going to do now?' was the frantic question in the All Black backline that showed our obsession with him.

Only very few players are like that because many of the 'tradesmen' who take the field are so utterly predictable, but not David. And so good was he at making me look something of a club player that a meeting was called and it was suggested Bernie and I swap wings. The reasoning was that Bernie, not scared of any physical confrontation, could 'soften' David up and then see how good he was. Fortunately it never came to that and I decided to meet him head on and battle it out. From what I can remember it was a fairly good clash. Ironically that physical, confrontational style never played a big role in David's makeup. He was more of a 'pure' winger where guile, speed, anticipation and style were more

With support from Jeff Miller, Campese evades
Ireland's Phil Matthews to score the first of his two
tries in the nail-biting 1991 World Cup quarter-final.

18

important than the crash, bang, take-it-up-the-guts style that's so prevalent.

It's a credit to David that he has outlasted his shelf life because a winger of his type should have been dead and buried long ago. He's the greatest 'touch' player we've seen—a genuine game-breaker with skills that most of us can only dream about.

But he's the last of his kind—the last of the great players who can claim membership of the original 'Wingers Club' where skill not size was the prerequisite for entry. Not anymore. Take a look at the last few years and see how the wingers have evolved. The John Kirwans and the Tuigamalas smashed onto the scene where subtlety played a secondary role. It was more the 'straight through' rather than 'glide around' approach that became the trademark of playing out wide. Now, of course, Jonah Lomu is taking that philosophy to a new level of sheer destruction. Very rarely do you see the deft overhead pass, the chip kick followed by the one-handed gathering of the ball, the swerve, the 'goose-step' or even a superbly thrown dummy. That's why David is so much of a rugby treasure—a living legend.

I must admit though that it always surprises me that he didn't play more at fullback. He was sensational out wide but I'm convinced he would have been better wearing the No.15 jersey more often. Just imagine how he could have attacked if he'd been given more chances at the back. He was safe under the high ball, had a strong boot, could step off both feet and despite a few missed tackles (something I can always relate to) was reasonable on defence. It's my humble opinion that his spontaneity and flamboyance would have been better suited there.

And he's still got the ability to surprise more than a decade later and he's still genuinely feared. That's the greatest compliment he can be paid because after watching him often, after analysing the videos, after discussing and dissecting his patterns he can still do something majestic. Even in the last few years I've said to myself after watching some of his magic, 'Only David could do that', or 'Hell, he's good.' He proved that with his sublime skills in beating the All Blacks in the World Cup semi-final in '91 where an overhead flick pass of 'out-of-this-world' quality and a scintillating try sunk our boys. That was David at his best.

But despite all the wondrous efforts on the field there's also been a few cock-ups. It's all part of the spell he weaves. Stuff-ups will occur when you're such a free spirit, but let's face it, he won't be ultimately remembered for those.

However, his on-the-field efforts don't tell the full story of the man. Along with every other New Zealand rugby fan I've always admired him because he brought the 'Fun Factor' into the game. And because of that and the intensity and pride he played with, he earned and then commanded the respect of the All Blacks and their fans.

Nothing ever seemed too much trouble for him and after intense games he's always gone out of his way to have a genuinely good time with his opponents. Over the years I've seen him quite a few times and it's never been one of those awkward sort of times you experience with some players. You know the sort of 'Ah hell there's so and so, I wonder what I'll say to him.' David's never been like that—there's never been an embarrassing or stilted conversation. It was like that when I was waiting at an airport in South Africa during the World Cup when I got a tap on the shoulder and turned around to see David. 'How are ya doing, Stu?' was the opening line and we took it from there as though we'd just stepped off the field after eighty minutes of combat. That genuine and sincere interest shows the quality of the bloke but to be honest that's how he deals with everyone, not just a former All Black winger.

I also reckon he should be regarded as rugby's first 'Freedom Fighter'. A bloke who fully embraced the 'professional' side of rugby long before it became acceptable and paved the way for the opportunities that far less gifted players have grasped with both hands. He led the fight against officialdom and his blunt, straight-shooting style didn't always make him 'Top of the Pops' with administrators but look what he achieved.

So how will he been seen in a hundred or so years? In my eyes he'll always be regarded as one of the game's geniuses. I'll always see him as a player of exceptional class and as a bloke you'd do anything for. In my book that's all you need.

'If you miss any more tackles, I'll take you off. I'd rather play with twelve.'
Queanbeyan rugby league coach, chastising a 15-year-old David Campese in 1977

THE FASTEST, MOST ELUSIVE WINGER IN THE WORLD

by Mark Ella

Former Australian captain Mark Ella and Campese played alongside each other in eighteen Tests before he retired, but his most enduring memory of Campese on the rugby field was one cold, wintry night in the southern NSW city of Wagga Wagga in 1986, or was it 1987?

On the charge for
Randwick against
Easts, Sydney grand
final 1991.

(below) Which way did he go? Grant Fox zigs when he should have zagged and Campo is off and running. Australia v New Zealand, Sydney, 1992.

(opposite) Just one more, fellas! Campese and Tim Horan pose with the prize after Australia's record-breaking 63-6 win over Wales at Ballymore in 1991.

t was a freezing cold night in Wagga Wagga some time back in 1986 or 1987 and there I was, five kilos overweight, preparing to play rugby again for an Invitation XV against a local regional side. I must have been mad. What makes anybody want to put their body through eighty minutes of torture, all for the fun of the game? I guess part of the rationale was the temptation of again playing with one of the greatest rugby players ever, my good friend David Campese. Campo was at the height of his career but I had retired in 1984 and my body shape had changed somewhat. However, I still thought I had it all until one particular moment when I was sprinting down the sideline and I looked inside to see if any of my teammates could keep up with me. Can you imagine my horror when I saw Tony Daly, a front row forward, running beside me without any effort at all? I was so distraught I simply passed him the ball and then sat back to watch him score his third try of the match. Immediately the truth hit me like a bolt of lightning: let somebody else do all the hard work and be there at the end for all the glory.

But what Campo did that night still remains firmly entrenched in my mind. It may not have happened against England or the All

Blacks, or for that matter Gordon, and how he did it was something you would have to see to believe. I was taking the ball up to the 22-metre line to restart play when I noticed Campo about three or four metres away to my left. I casually turned to face him and knew instinctively he wanted me to play him the ball. After looking right (as one would expect from a left-footed kicker), I deftly placed a right-footed drop kick to Campo on my left. He took the ball on the fly and because I was a little incapable of following the fastest, most elusive rugby back in the world, I left him to do all the work.

Campo took off to the left, beating most of the bigger forwards, before stepping off his left foot, back right to beat the back row. Near the halfway mark he decided to go back out to evade a couple of the inside backs, whom he beat easily, then he came back infield in case the faster players ran him down, with a couple of quick steps, a couple of in-and-aways, the odd side-step and maybe even a goose-step thrown in, just to please the crowd. He had beaten fourteen players from a set phase and as he neared their 22-metre line all he had in front of him was one worried full-back who knew what was coming.

What do you think I was doing all this time apart from watching the show? I had stumbled down the centre of the field minding my own business when my moment of glory arrived. Campo spared the fullback any indignity in front of his home gathering and passed the ball inside, gratefully received by one fat five-eighth who scored underneath the posts. Most of the applause was, as usual, for Campo.

I doubt the world will ever see a player like David Campese again. As he enters the twilight of his career, most of the talk is centred around his heir apparent, Jonah Lomu. It's true Lomu will be the next star of international rugby but believe me when I say he is definitely not the next David Campese.

Campo could and still can do anything. He can run, step, caress, kick, outwit and out-think the best of them. Part of assessing a worthy opponent or adversary is to try and find out what he's thinking. Trying to outsmart Campo is pointless because he has so many natural and instinctive talents to call upon. Jonah, at this stage of his career, doesn't use too much objective thinking apart from running over the top of opponents in a manner never seen in rugby before.

Campo will never be replaced in my mind as being one of the greatest ever. He never gives up hope of winning even when the odds are against him. I loved playing rugby with him because, like me, he always wanted to attack. He possessed this trait when he first toured with the Wallabies in New Zealand in 1982 and to this day that hasn't changed.

Our 1984 tour of Great Britain and Ireland will always be remembered in Australian rugby history and for me it was special because I had the opportunity to play attacking rugby at the highest level. Playing alongside Campo made it particularly special because we did it together, like two revolutionaries winning the war. We both feel that at the end of the day the style in which the game is won is often more important than winning.

Whether he should have retired after the 1995 World Cup in South Africa will be one of the most contentious points in Campo's career. I don't know what keeps him going—I hope it's not the sight of my expanding waistline! Whatever it is, only David knows. If he truly believes that he still possesses the ability and determination to carry on, then good luck to him. I hope that wanting to be the first, and probably only, Wallaby to play 100 Tests for his country is his motivation. Athletes should play their

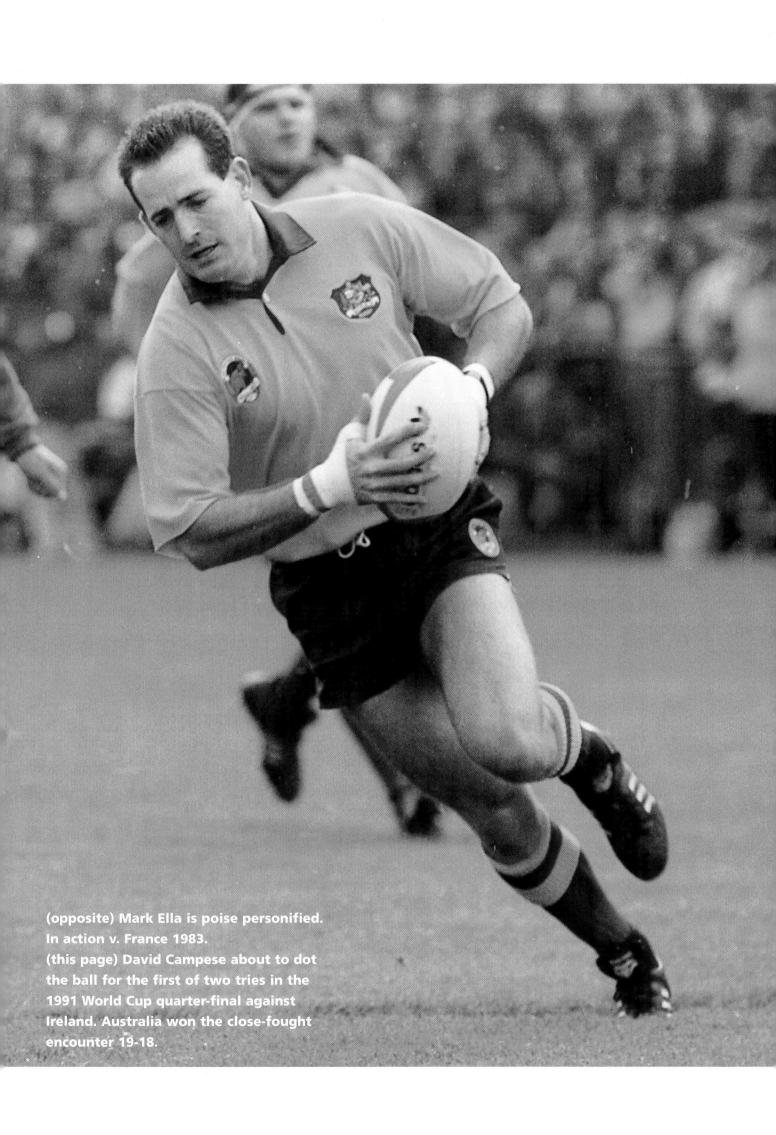

(opposite) Mark Ella is poise personified.
In action v. France 1983.
(this page) David Campese about to dot
the ball for the first of two tries in the
1991 World Cup quarter-final against
Ireland. Australia won the close-fought
encounter 19-18.

chosen sport because of the love of it first and foremost. Sometimes the financial rewards can be a motivation but I hope that in David's case, it isn't that rugby has become his life and that all else revolves around it. If that is so, then I would urge him to retire because there is definitely life after rugby.

When I look back on David's career, it's hard to believe that he's been around for so long. I remember him and all his hair when he scored his first Test try against New Zealand at Lancaster Park in Christchurch in 1982. I remember when he beat Miguens, the Argentinian fullback in 1983 at the Sydney Cricket Ground using the goose-step to score another try. I recall that try against the Barbarians in 1984 and I especially remember Campo being the first by my side when, against Scotland, I scored my fourth Test try of the tour. I remember him being lampooned by Alan Jones in New Zealand in 1986 when he was wrongly accused of losing the Test match, and being boxed in by seven Barbarian players in 1988 and beating all seven of them. I was co-commentating with Nigel Starmer-Smith in 1989 when Campo threw a pass to nobody, giving the British Lions winger Ieuan Evans a match and series winning try. I remember Campo flicking the ball over his shoulder for Tim Horan to score a try against New Zealand in the semi-final of the 1991 World Cup, the tournament that clearly established him as the best in the world. David was at my side as a close friend to me and my family when I was coaching in Milan and I remember him last year, when the rugby world was starting to have second thoughts on his ability to continue playing at the top.

All of those memories give me a great insight into a very complex human being. He isn't the easiest person to get to know, but once you do, his loyalty and friendship are bountiful.

I hope my memories of David Campese in 1996 will be just as vivid in years to come.

(below) With Mark Ella enjoying the Italian experience.

'There is something about Campese that upsets people. When he makes mistakes people never forgive him. Somehow Campo's astonishing record of try-scoring is overlooked.'

Nick Farr-Jones

THE BRADMAN OF RUGBY UNION

by Alan Jones

Broadcaster and former Wallaby coach, Alan Jones was there when the Campese legend began. And he talks about the hallmarks of the expression of the Campese genius.

Hearts swell with pride as the
National Anthem rings out. Before
Australia v Fiji, second Test.
Sydney Cricket Ground, 1985.

t's valid to argue that whole forests have been cut down as writers, commentators and critics across the rugby world have sought to define the almost indefinable qualities of David Campese. I once said he was the Bradman of rugby union and it's not a judgement from which I would ever resile. For the bulk of his rugby career, Campese, ball in hand, or even the anticipation of Campese receiving the football, brought people to their feet. I was at the Sydney Cricket Ground in 1982 when this unknown Canberra teenage fullback was playing in what was regarded as something of a trial, a curtain raiser to a Test against a New Zealand Under 21 side, though rarely did anyone from such a trial graduate immediately to much else. People were wandering into the ground and those who were there gave little attention to what was happening on the paddock. But on this day, and not for the first time, a remarkably gifted and fleet of foot Canberra teenager swept into the back line, received the ball at the end of a pass, chip-kicked, accelerated, gathered and scored.

It's the sort of stuff you joke about with a few beers under your belt, the fantasy that most people aspire to convert into reality. With David Campese, it was the beginning of a phenomenal career because, fortunately, some important people were watching. Campo went straight into the Australian team to go to New Zealand and has never looked back.

(left) Campo the Barbarian, 1990. (below) Off and running, with Phil Matthews chasing and Simon Poidevin and Jeff Miller in support. World Cup quarter-final v Ireland, 1991.

He ran rings around every opponent even then, mesmerising the best, disillusioning the not-so-good and destroying the mediocre. If Campese has been the Bradman of rugby union, he is also the David Copperfield. Just as the remarkable illusionist conjures things out of nothing, tempts the imagination and, to the naked eye, does the impossible, so too does Campese.

One of the weaknesses of a Campese critique is that it's fashionable and part of the Australian character to dwell upon his omissions. There have been flaws along the way. I am sure that when he played for me, during my time as Australian coach, there were moments when he frustrated more than fascinated me. But I have to be truthful. I can't immediately remember. I do remember him irritating me one day with carelessness at training, in 1987 I think, at Trinity Grammar. And I shouted at him, more than I should have, and in a language more strident than perhaps was necessary.

I also remember us playing the All Blacks in the wet in 1986 at Eden Park in our remarkable Bledisloe Cup tour and Campo was running off his own line in defence. I always said that when in the wet the blind side was your friend. And rightly, true to script, Campo came off his own line, ball in hand, and headed to the blind side.

(above) Campo and the coach. Under Alan Jones in 1986, Australia won a series in New Zealand for only the second time.
(below) The Bledisloe Cup, symbol of trans-Tasman rugby rivalry since 1931.

(right) Campese pursued by All Black captain Gary Whetton (centre) and Sean Fitzpatrick (right), moments before he scores the first try in the World Cup semi-final, **1991.**

(above) Alan Jones, 1986.

But he had a habit of adding to the script. It was the very quality which, most times, defined his greatness. But on this occasion, my heart leapt and our collective hopes sank as Campo hurled a 'Hail Mary' pass inside to be intercepted by New Zealand who scored beside the posts. Suddenly, a winning lead and victory were both at peril, but we survived. The next night at a happy hour with the team, we had a concert where everybody had to put on an act. Steve Cutler chose a Wallabies' version of 'Sale of The Century' and the first question was 'Who scored two tries at Eden Park on Saturday?' Now at first thought no-one did, because the score was 13–12 to us. But Cuts' answer was 'Campo. He scored one for us and one for them!'

When David was down later in his career and I had ceased coaching Australia he actually retired. I remember speaking at the launch of his biography and telling him and the hundreds who were present that he hadn't sought permission from us!

I chastised him constantly about dwelling on the mistakes he's made and warned him that the press would do that better than he could and more often. He should dwell upon the strengths instead.

He has made a remarkable comeback from those deeply depressing times. His performance at the 1991 World Cup was phenomenal—without him and the incredible Michael Lynagh, Australia would have sunk without a trace. Now Campese knows that wherever the history of rugby is written, the name Campese will be in bold print.

I remember before we played Scotland at Murrayfield in 1984

in the final leg of what we hoped would be a Grand Slam triumph, I challenged the team to make sure that they became a headline rather than a footnote in the history of the game. Campese has not only accepted the challenge since then but comprehensively delivered on it.

What has been the key to this success and the remarkable place David Campese occupies in the affections of those who love the sport? Well, there are many. I would say first, an often unacknowledged single-mindedness—his sitting at the front of the bus is a metaphor of his life, he aims never to be behind.

He's looked after himself and he's a super athlete, blessed with speed not so much as acceleration. And he's got the feet, the co-ordination, the timing and the judgement that mark out all great sports people. There have been many electrifying moments in the career and there have been equally many of us who've suffered as a result of his sometimes loose tongue—even Campo has been known to confuse fact with fiction! But none of us should be able to quibble about that.

The overall impression he leaves is a sense of extraordinary exhilaration and we have often felt overwhelmed at his accomplishments. We have been frustrated, but that has been overtaken by the satisfaction shared by those of us who have travelled part of the road with him, that we were there when the Campese history was being written.

In particular, I shall never forget the Barbarians game at Cardiff Arms Park to end our Grand Slam tour of 1984. We weren't in such good shape—our discipline had surrendered to celebration after beating Scotland and we knew this was to be Europe's game of retribution against us. We seemed to be constantly counter-attacking to get out of trouble and then Campese struck. He made a break from inside his own half, the defence came at him and he stepped left and right with remarkable speed. And in the twinkling of an eye, the try line was his.

But he had one defender to beat, the Welsh centre Robert Ackerman. Ackerman, unfortunately, had criticised the Australian backline after our crushing victory in the Test against Wales and Campo didn't have the words to retaliate then. But he retaliated now, with his feet and hands.

He turned Ackerman inside out, threatening to go past, then changing direction, offering himself to be tackled then accelerating away until the crowd erupted, first in disbelief, then in sheer amusement and joy at what they were seeing.

One yard from the line, Campo passed to Michael Hawker, and I'm sure, to this day, the pass was forward, but the referee knew he had seen artistry of incomparable dimension at work and the only reward he could offer was a try, which he duly did.

It's an image I'll always associate with David Campese.

It remains for me the metaphor of his career.

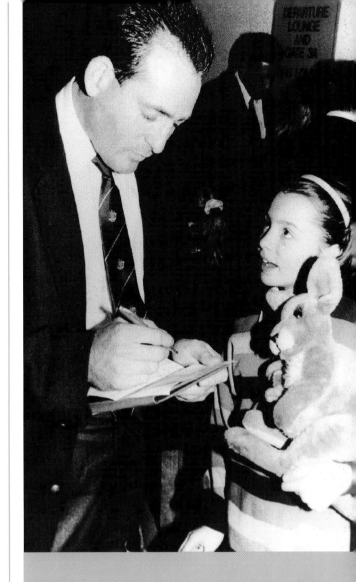

'He's the Maradona, the Pele of international rugby all rolled into one.'

Irish Test great Tony Ward, after Australia's 16–6 win over New Zealand in the semi-final of the 1991 World Cup

INTUITIVE, INSPIRATIONAL, INCOMPARABLE

by Peter Jenkins

Peter Jenkins, rugby writer for the Australian *newspaper since 1991, evokes the late inventor Thomas Alva Edison to define the inspiration Campese brings to the game.*

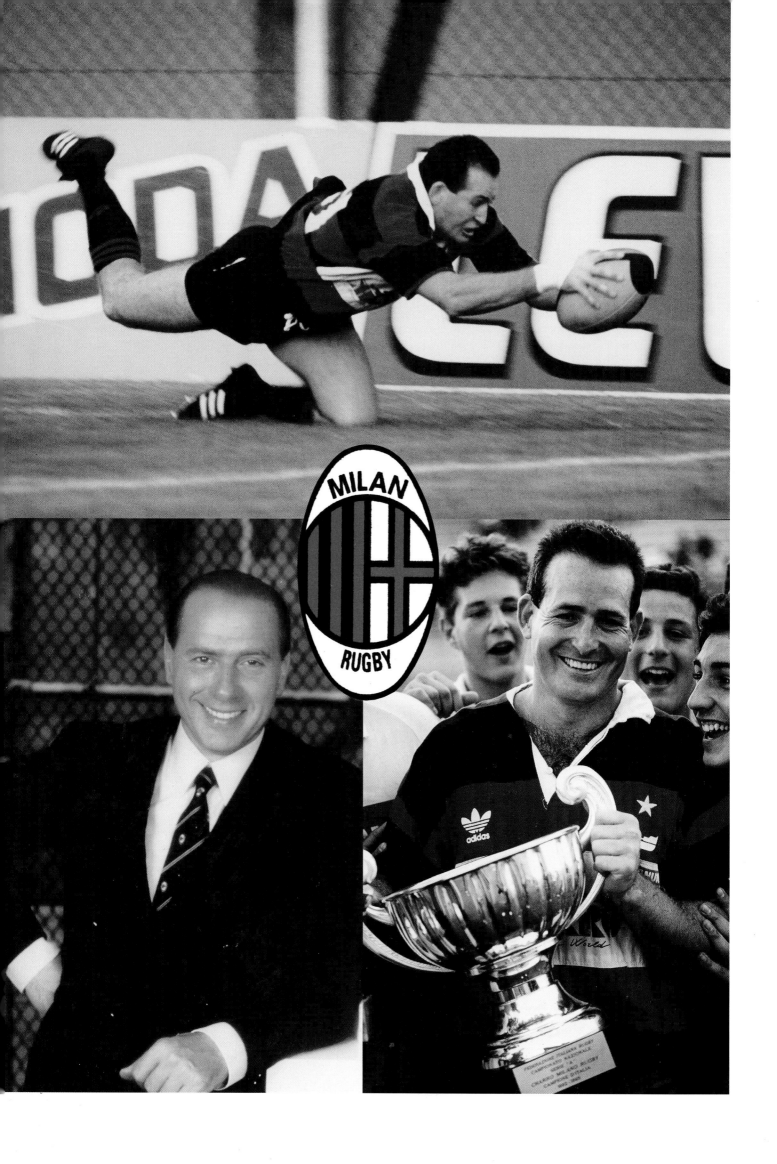

Around the turn of the century, Thomas Edison, American inventor and father of the light bulb, was asked to define genius. It was, he suggested, one per cent inspiration, ninety-nine per cent perspiration. If Edison was alive today, if he was a rugby union devotee, if he had witnessed the career of David Campese, he may feel tempted to revise those figures. Inspiration might just be worth a few more percentage points.

The intuitive reactions, the messages relayed from brain to feet without the need for thought. No amount of sweat could hone the instinctive gifts, and they are considerable, that Campese has brought to the game. His weaving run for the Australians against the Barbarians at Cardiff Arms Park in 1988, when the crowd rose as one and his own teammates applauded him back to halfway. The over-the-shoulder pass to teammate Tim Horan, without so much as a glance in his direction, for a try against the All Blacks in the World Cup semi-final of 1991. His trademark goosestep. They are all defining features of a player whose talents have set him apart.

But the Edison premise, that it takes more than a flash of brilliance to mould genius, still applies to Campese. He has always trained to entertain, and rarely misses a day of rehearsal. Those one-handed pick-ups at full pace, when the ball is bobbling across the turf. Campese practises them. First with his right hand, then with his left. On his own at a local park. The chip and chase routine. Practices that too, while his home away from home, for many years, has been the gym. Fitness and skills have not been taken for granted.

Nearing his mid-thirties, that approach has become a necessity, but Campese has followed the same routine throughout most of his rugby career. It annoys him that others, younger than he, are reluctant to follow the lead. 'There are those who would presume a lot of my success has been based on natural ability,' he says. 'That's a myth. Part of the reason I have got a carefree attitude on the pitch is because I know I've done the work.'

Edison would be pleased.

The Campese work ethic is tied to his oft-quoted line that rugby union is his life. The words might sound trite—a romantic, over-the-top assessment of a player and his sporting pursuit. But in Campese's case, it's true. The two are indelibly tied, even to the extent that personal relationships have struggled to compete with his obsession for the game. He was engaged once, has had several steady girlfriends. But rugby was always priority one, and his boots a passport to travel.

For many years, his lifestyle involved dividing his time between the winters of Italy and Australia. Such an existence is hardly conducive to maintaining long-term relationships. What Campese

(opposite at top) In action for Milano.
(bottom left) Italian media magnate and owner of the Milano rugby team, Silvio Berlusconi.
(bottom right) Enjoying the Italian first division `Serie A' trophy.

43

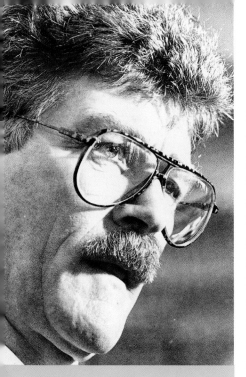

has continued is an ongoing affair with the game he first played in his youth, growing up in the working-class town of Queanbeyan, near the Australian Capital Territory. A game that has earned him celebrity status and wealth, and the occasional heartache.

He still, for instance, cringes when reminded of that infamous pass near his own line in the third Test against the British Lions in 1989, when Welsh winger Ieuan Evans pounced on the loose ball to score a decisive try. Campese was devastated, his fragile frame of mind not helped later by what he perceived, mostly imagined, as post-match rejection from teammates and pressmen. He will tell you, seven years later, that the only person to offer words of consolation in the dressing-room after the game was coach Bob Dwyer. Feeling like an outcast, Campese stayed only briefly at the function that followed the Test. Driving home he was pulled over for speeding. It wasn't his day.

He was living at the time with his friends Daryl and Julie McGraw in a leafy suburb on Sydney's north shore. The McGraws are Campese's confidants, his business partners and, in many respects, his extended family. The night of the British Lions Test they recall how, totally out of character, he drank a bottle of liqueur.

Campese enjoys the occasional glass of wine, his Italian heritage demands it. But rarely anything more. He dislikes the taste of beer and never sips anything more potent than water, soft drink or juice in the dressing-room after a match. When interviewing Campese for *My Game Your Game*, a book he co-produced with former Australian rugby league captain Mal Meninga, he made the point: 'I'm not a big drinker and never have been... I suppose that's the reason I don't seem to socialise very well after games. I can't stand around talking, having drink after drink in a bar. I would rather an orange juice or two and go home.'

In Swansea, Wales, in 1992, when the Wallabies were on tour, a local nightclub, Barons, was the meeting place for the Australian players the night after their match. Campese turned up late, and would have stayed no more than half an hour. Three media representatives, ice packs to aching heads the next day, wished they had done the same.

(below) Wrapped in ribbons and glad of it—Phil Kearns and Campese at the World Cup ticker-tape parade, 1991. (above right) Australian Rugby Union president Joe French is neatly framed by David Campese and Nick Farr-Jones as they hold the 1991 World Cup aloft.

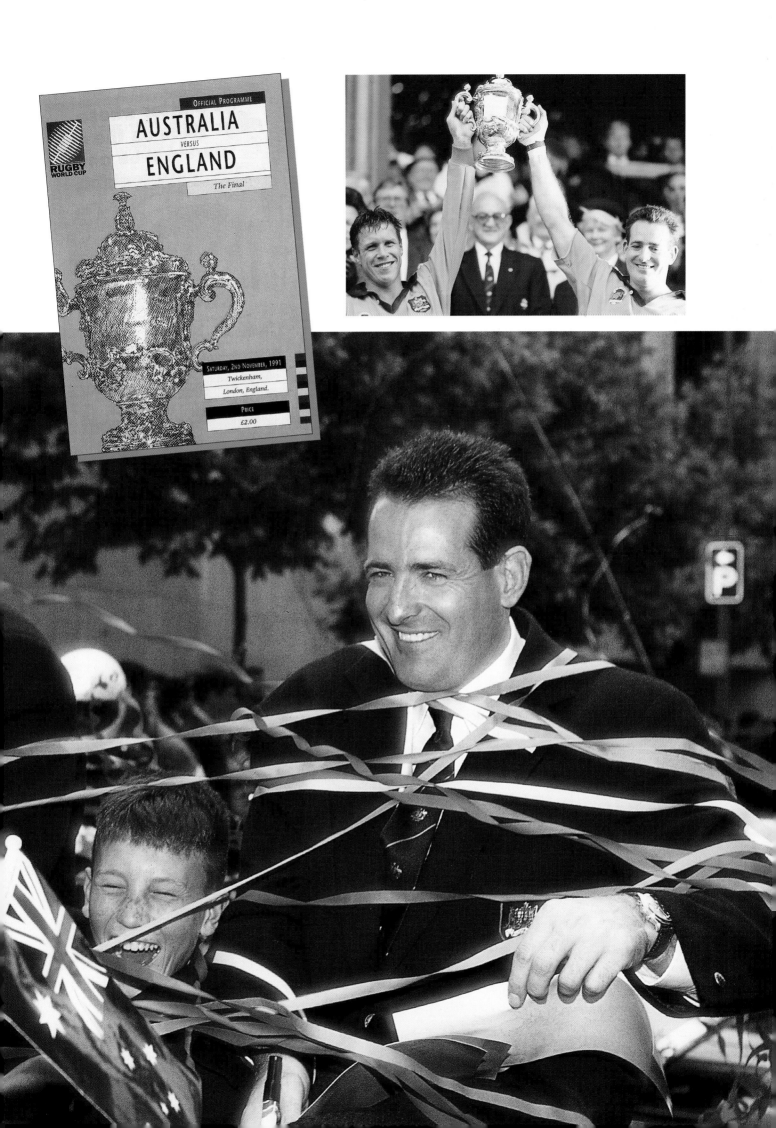

Avoiding alcohol, and those filled with it, is not uncommon for Campese. And it shows how deeply the Lions had clawed when he threw a few down on the night of that series decider.

The following day I knocked on the door of the McGraw residence, having arranged to interview Campese. It was early afternoon and he told how he felt like retiring. As we talked, he stood in the kitchen, wearing a t-shirt and bike shorts, stirring pasta sauce and boiling fettuccine. As the week wore on, much of the criticism directed his way was, he believed, excessive. He argued that other crucial mistakes were made in the game. Besides, he said, his game, by nature, involved an element of risk. If he had taken the conservative route all his life, his try-scoring deeds would have been curbed dramatically. Campese was wounded and, even today, scars remain from 1989.

For despite the on-field showmanship, the confidence to try what others would not and the verbal bravado—he speaks his mind and to hell with diplomacy—there is another side to Campese. If you prick him, he does bleed, and Campese can be sensitive, as many others are, to unfavourable press. He can brood about criticism, either written or spoken, like a child chastised by an aunt. The body language, at times, is unmistakable. But, for the most part, Campese enjoys being in the media spotlight, despite what he says about never reading papers. The media enjoys it too. Forget political correctness, and bland sporting clichés. If Campese has an opinion to express, prepare the sub-editors. It's time to write those headlines.

When the Australians arrived in South Africa to play the

Springboks on their return from isolation in 1992, Campese told the local press the Wallabies should not have had to make the trip. As world champions, they should have made the Springboks travel. His prospects of a diplomatic posting to Pretoria slumped. They were buried a short time later when he slated Springbok legend Naas Botha. Campese claimed that in all his years in Italy, where Botha also played club rugby, he had never seen the South African make a tackle. A number of South African journalists sat open-mouthed in disbelief. His outspoken comments annoy officials, they can get up the nose of his fellow players, and have put offside more than one coach. Controversy is something Campese has never attempted, or never been able, to goosestep.

But while tact may not be his strong point, what of the alternative? Another sporting automaton, programmed to spit out the sterile replies: 'We'll take it match by match' or the classic 'It's a funny game.' Campese has opened his mouth at the wrong times, shot from the hip and been wrong. But on other occasions he's been close to the mark, as well as close to the bone. He complained about the Wallabies' style of play—'it never gets to the wings'—long before the 1995 World Cup. After the tournament, Tim Horan and Jason Little joined the chorus.

We were speaking about that same issue at a restaurant in Cape Town, a few days after the Wallabies had been beaten by England in the quarter-finals. The conversation, though, never went far. An endless stream of fellow diners approached the table, napkins in hand, wanting the Campese autograph. He obliged everyone, even the boorish middle-aged gent whose request went along the lines of 'sign this'. That he did was typical Campese.

Acutely aware of his profile, Campese has never been one for the 'superstar snub'—the nose in the air and push your way past the adoring masses routine. More often than not, after a match, he can still be seen out on the field, signing autographs, when others are back in the dressing room. There is a sense of duty about it, but also a sense of decency, a Campese character trait that can appear at odds with the acid-tongued barbs he's been known to fire at rivals and officials.

I recall our first interview for *My Game Your Game*. We had agreed to meet at the waterfront unit he was staying in at the time. Showing my usual regard for punctuality, I arrived twenty minutes late. I know, because Campese, a stickler for those sort of things, told me. But on learning I had not eaten, he offered to prepare a quick breakfast. Tomato on toast? Fine. It was served neatly cut in quarters. He even brushed the crumbs off the bench. It was a job that required ninety-nine per cent perspiration. But his culinary effort—it tasted like any other tomato on toast—did not have the hallmark of genius.

Campese saves that for the rugby paddock, and there'll be many who will miss it when it's gone.

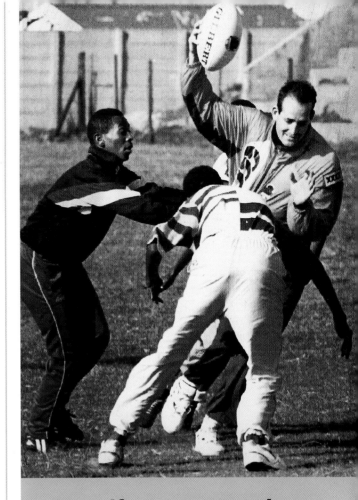

Now if you want a player who just never makes a blue The flying wing Campese may not be the man for you But if you want a player who can set the place alight Then Campo is the man to call, he's simply dynamite.
Peter Fenton

(opposite at top) A happy snap with Wallaby teammates before the World Cup final, 1991. The tip doing the rounds among the Aussie players was that if they wanted to get their pictures in the papers ... just get close to Campo!
(opposite at bottom) Australia v England, 1995 World Cup quarter-final.
(above) Campo shows off his skills to youngsters at a coaching clinic in the black township of Zwide, near Port Elizabeth, South Africa.

ENTERTAINER PAR EXCELLENCE

by Bill McLaren

*Scottish television commentator Bill McLaren
remembers some of Campese's great matches on
three tours of the United Kingdom and Ireland.
A few in particular were played in Melrose in
the Scottish border country, birthplace of
seven-a-side rugby.*

49

(above) Meeting the Queen, with skipper Nick Farr-Jones handling the formalities. Before the kickoff, 1991 World Cup final at Twickenham.
(opposite at top) In action against the Barbarians in 1984. Australia won 37-30.
(opposite at bottom) Randwick v Gordon, 1990—Campese has winger Alistair Murdoch at bay with Matt Dixon struggling to bring him down.

hen I last saw David Campese during the New South Wales tour to Scotland in February 1996 I was of the view that it might be the last time that we would meet as player and commentator as each was in the eventide of his career, although I would delight to see him reach his personal milestone of 100 caps.

So it was in Edinburgh, where in 1984 he had brought the Murrayfield crowd to its feet with a vintage performance culminating in a typically gorgeous try, that I caused him some embarrassment by thanking him for the vast pleasure he had given me in commentary at matches in which he had been involved. I really meant that accolade because, having been fortunate enough to have seen all the truly class players since I entered into the commentary field in 1952, I have no hesitation in saying that no player ever made commentary a greater pleasure than David Campese. He has been a commentator's dream.

The quality of commentary depends to a large extent upon the quality of play on the field. Once I was calling a Scotland v Wales game at Murrayfield in which there were 111 lineouts! They reckoned that Wales had six different code words and each meant kick for touch! Trying to encourage viewer interest in that war of attrition up and down the touch lines really was heavy going. Had David Campese been playing in that game he would have given the forwards and halves a piece of his mind because there was no way that he would remain unemployed on the wing without expressing an opinion in very forthright terms.

In an age where the game and its participants have become so predictable, when it is possible to forecast with some assurance exactly what any given player will do in specific circumstances, it has been both refreshing and a delight to come across one who was just different, who sometimes didn't know himself what he would do, far less anyone else! Talk about being unorthodox, a law unto himself or whatever, David Campese is an entertainer par excellence because he doesn't conform but provides joyous spells of the unexpected in tilting his lance, sometimes in an audacious and outrageous fashion. He could prove to be the last of a dying breed of adventurers. Of course he knew when a touch of percentage rugby was required. His instinctive feel for what was on saw to that. But he is so gifted with flair and vision as to frequently make a little go a long way. A little space was all he required to display his unusual command of the arts of deception, of swerve, sidestep, feint, pace change and even of hand-off as well as adhesive hands and variations in weight, shape and direction of pass. He could kick a bit as well! He and Mike Gibson of Ireland are the most complete footballers I have ever seen. Either could have played in any back division position in an international and still would have made a huge impact.

Apart from the fillip he provided for the commentator with that adventurous style, there were also delightful bits from the David Campese biographical information that helped to decorate commentary and provide additional interest for listeners and viewers. There was, for instance, that deceptive running hitch-kick he used to check opponents. Some called it the 'Struggletown Shuffle' and I enjoyed using that description in commentary. Unfortunately most of the youngsters I coached as a teacher of physical education tried to copy the shuffle and more often than not, tripped over their feet in the process! They all wanted to be David Campese but they weren't as good at it as 'Himself'.

I also used to enjoy telling viewers about the restaurateur in David's old stamping ground, Queanbeyan, who so appreciated the great man's play and the influence he had on putting Queanbeyan firmly on the map, that he named a special dish 'Fillet Campese'. How many rugby men have been paid that kind of a compliment?

Whenever David Campese played there was a kind of electric expectancy in the air and in all the times I have seen him in action, the audience was never disappointed. Of course he has endeared himself to my fellow countrymen by his frank and outspoken comments about the style of play embraced by England! But even before that he had become a favourite with Scots who revelled in his exciting style even though it was often to the detriment of the home sides. The climax to Australia's Grand Slam success in the United Kingdom in 1984 took place at Murrayfield and I can still

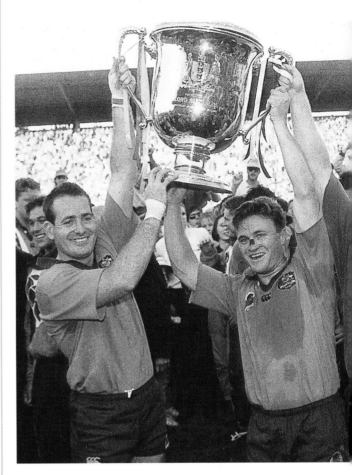

(opposite at top) Campese offloads to Tim Horan (No.12), Australia v England, Sydney, 1991.

(above) Campese and Paul Carozza with the Bledisloe Cup after Australia's 19-17 win at Ballymore, 1992.

see him joining a counter-attack from his own '22', igniting Steve Tuynman, gathering in Tuynman's inside pass then taking off at such a rate of knots that John Beattie, a British Lion in New Zealand in 1983, just never looked like preventing him from scoring. The great man was accorded a massive ovation from the Murrayfield crowd.

There was another ovation, just as deafening, at Cardiff Arms Park in 1988 at the climax to the traditional end-of-tour Barbarians match. David Campese capped an exhilarating Australian performance with a gem of a try when he glided outside Gavin Hastings, swept inside Matt Duncan then, with a feint off his right foot and one off his left foot, he left Jonathan Davies trailing in his wake before dotting down behind the posts. It was a masterpiece of deceptive running and it brought from the Cardiff Arms Park audience the most moving acknowledgment of sheer wizardry that I can ever remember. The ovation lasted for ages and I can remember my own reaction: 'Sheer genius from the moment he received the ball. The great swashbuckler has rung down the curtain with the touch of a magician.'

To see David Campese in seven-a-side play was another delight. The abbreviated version seemed to be made for him. Of course it was invented near my own home area of the Scottish border country at Melrose and there was massive interest in the appearance of David Campese in the Randwick squad who were special guests in 1990 at the 'Blue Riband' of the spring sevens series, the Melrose tournament. Came the day and the rain simply

teemed down on a pitch that was treacherous to say the least. The local players rubbed their hands in gleeful anticipation. Here was the weather and ground conditions to which they were accustomed and in which they could revel. Such hazardous conditions would cut the famous Wallaby down to size. The Borderers would show the great man how it should be done. Some hope! He was the star of the show, the tournament's top try-scorer and points-scorer with 44 of Randwick's 92 points. Not only that but he was like a duck in water, completely at home, fizzing about in the 'glaur', the Border name for cloying mud, as to the manner born. He had been preparing himself for water sports having previously asked that his Melrose billet should have a swimming pool! He saved Randwick from semi-final defeat with a typical touch of Campese magic. Randwick were 15–12 in arrears to Melrose with time almost up when he received the ball at halfway and took off like an inebriated skater. Some metres short of the goal line he produced a dive that would have done credit to an Olympic swimmer and slithered his way to a momentous try that took Randwick to the final in which they beat the renowned sevens artistes from Kelso who included the famous 'White Shark', John Jeffrey. David admitted afterwards that he was grateful for the rain and mud: 'I wouldn't have scored that try on a dry day because I would not have been able to aquaplane into the corner.'

It may come as a surprise that David has a taste for Hawick Bells. They are hard-boiled mint sweets manufactured in my own home town of Hawick. When I gave him one for the very first time his reaction was: 'Will I pass a bloody drug test with one of those inside me?'

I asked my wife, Bette, and our daughters Linda and Janie, what kind of impression David Campese had made upon them. The consensus amounted to this: 'He epitomises the fun and excitement that the game should always have on offer. He plays the game the way womenfolk would want it to be played having regard to the fact that some women do not know a great deal about the finer points. They naturally react to a handsome fellow running with the ball in an artful way just like poetry in motion. The rugby world has been much richer because David Campese has been part of it.'

Once, when I asked Wallaby coach Bob Dwyer how he set about coaching David Campese he replied: 'Bill, I make it a point never to interfere with true genius.' That surely says it all.

David Ian, I salute you in appreciation and with my thanks for all the pleasure you have given me as a Scottish commentator revelling in a genuine class act demonstrating all the arts and crafts in a thoroughly entertaining manner.

Buona Fortuna for your century.

(above) A rugby tradition—the Hong Kong Sevens.
(inset) The Webb Ellis Trophy— awarded to the champions of the rugby world every four years.

'He's the sort of player whose brain doesn't always know where his legs are carrying him.'
Nick Farr-Jones

LEGENDS SHOOT STRAIGHT FROM THE HIP

by Tracey Holmes

ABC Radio sports commentator and presenter of Grandstand Tracey Holmes has always enjoyed Campese's outspokenness and the havoc he creates off the field.

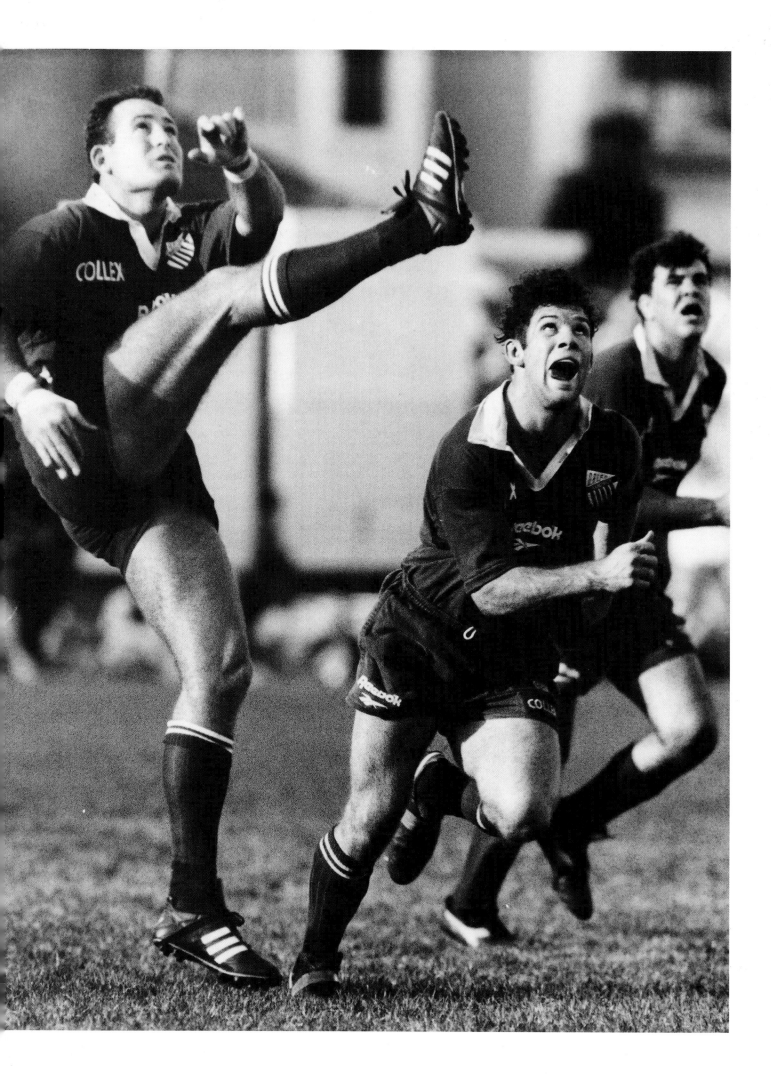

(left) It's high enough to bring rain. David Kelaher (centre) and Michael Cheika (right) follow a Campese skyscraper for Randwick.

(above) Campese tackles New Zealand fullback Kieran Crowley during the 1991 World Cup semi-final against New Zealand.

What can you say about Campo that hasn't already been said? He's done it all, he's played it all and he's certainly said it all. From the first moment Campo was recognised as a star he has been advised at regular intervals, by people who want to mould the champion into something he isn't, to just play the game and keep his mouth shut. I, for one, am glad he's ignored the advice. While the do-gooders are happy to watch this magician wave his magic spell over every aspect of the game— his team, the opponents and the crowd—I much prefer to absorb the havoc he creates off the park.

David Campese—honest, open, frank. A former Wallaby coach once said that there is a long winding path between a thought's birthplace and our mouths, whereas Campo thinks straight from his mouth. And good on him. Instead of running around wearing his No.11 jersey and trying to look like him, why don't we run around thinking from our mouths and trying to act like him? Do you know why?

Because it takes guts to think from the mouth and not too many of us are that gutsy. When Campo thinks the selectors treat him harshly he tells them. And he tells us. When he thinks the game has gone wrong, he tells the coach and his teammates, and again, he takes us into his confidence. How many players do you know that offer a free invitation to come and have a look at the

59

truth inside their heads? There's only one, and that's David Campese.

Campo is the one bloke we can rely on to take us right onto the field to play the game with him. Racing down the touchline we're out of breath. We gulp for air every time he pauses before performing that incredible goose-step. We shout to the skies whenever he scores a try and we damn the earth whenever his kicks go astray. We live every moment with one of the greatest wingers of all time. Campo isn't just Campo—he is all of us, the good, the bad and the ugly. He is the genius, he is the dunce. He is praised for winning games and bagged for losing them.

Campo has the widest shoulders of any man I've ever known, figuratively speaking, because he has to shoulder it all. A whole team contests the World Cup, a plethora of coaches and minders to help, yet if we lose, it's because Campo's rhythm had deserted him and left him like a drunken busker without a tune. Equally, though, if we win it's most likely due to just one dreamlike

(above left) It was something to celebrate–Campo's fiftieth Test try— and Ewan McKenzie and Tony Daly shared the moment after the Australia v South Africa game, Cape Town, 1992.
(above right) Campese in full flight in the second Test against New Zealand, Sydney, 1995.
(right) The Australian hordes close in to try and stop the unstoppable Jonah Lomu. Australia v New Zealand, Sydney, 1995.

moment when Campo danced like an angel across the heavens.

What about after the game, when all the other players give us their same old lines about taking it one match at a time and doing it for the team. What a load of rot. No-one does it one game at a time, there's always an ulterior motive—like the premiership or the Bledisloe Cup or the Webb Ellis Trophy. And as for doing it for the rest of the team, they've got to be kidding! It's a dog-eat-dog world out there on the sports ground and every bloke is thinking selfishly about his own performance and commercial value. Do you really think a broken down has-been who's fighting to retain his position for the next tour really gives a damn about his teammates? It's a shallow statement. See-through quotes like that would never be uttered by Campo. He always comes out with a clanger, something that makes us gasp while the officials cringe.

They say actions speak louder than words. Well, the philosopher that came up with that little gem wasn't around in the Campo era. His actions speak loudly, very loudly indeed, especially

when a stadium full of fans bursts into song the moment the ball is delivered into his great hands...but his words are like manna from heaven, everybody wants to hear what the god of rugby has to say. His quotes are splashed from one side of the globe to the other, they invoke retaliation of the most aggressive kind and controversy is but a path paved in his wake. And like all other gods, he walks on regardless, unaware of the mayhem he leaves behind. Yes, I think I've put my finger on it. Campo is deep, his messages often veiled and difficult to grasp, but surely this is just testimony to the awesome creation he is. When Campo finally hangs up his boots, rugby will be a lesser game—no inspiration, no goose-steps, no flamboyance on the field and no creative talking off it.

Love the guy or hate him, you will be passionate about him. There is nothing lukewarm about Campo. While his talent has earned him worldwide adoration, his arrogance could earn him the Australian prime ministership one day. And his looks...well, they could probably earn him something also. They probably already have!

(above) Campese in try-scoring mode. Australia v Fiji, Sydney Cricket Ground, 1985.
(below) Coach Bob Dywer ponders an eleven points loss to New Zealand after the second Test in Sydney, 1995. That day marked the only time in his Test career that Campese ran on as a replacement.

'The world is getting so dull and rugby is getting so dull. The player who can attack and through sheer ability make a crowd stand on its feet is very rare. To do the things Campo does is a special gift. Later on, Campese should be kept in some sort of a glass cage for teaching purposes.'

Former Wallaby captain Mark Loane

A RUGBY GOD IN THE NORTHERN HEMISPHERE

by Stephen Jones

David Campese was one of the stand-out players on the 1984 Wallaby 'Grand Slam' tour of Great Britain, but it was during the following tour in 1988 that he achieved the mantle of greatness among British fans of the game, writes Stephen Jones, rugby writer for London's Sunday Times.

Action Man, with a ball in his hand.
Running it for NSW v Queensland.

65

(left) Irish prop Nick Popplewell strains to arrest a charging Campese. Australia v Barbarians, 1992.
(above) Wearing a South African jersey and his biggest smile after the fiftieth Test try. In Cape Town, 1992.

When Australia came to the United Kingdom for their tour of 1988, David Campese was already established as a rugby player of the very top class. He had already been crowned the 'Bradman of rugby' by Alan Jones, the former Australian national coach. Yet although he had been playing Test matches for Australia for nearly six years, he was not so well appreciated in Britain. He had not yet, in British eyes, earned the right to be called vintage, all-time great.

He was not yet held in the combination of awe and affection which was later lavished the man. He had simply not been seen here enough; 1988 was still in those far-off, pre-satellite TV days too, when Down Under Tests were served up in the British Isles only in short dribs and drabs. He had played a leading role in the 1984 Grand Slam Wallaby tour, but due to the almost terminally dreadful state of rugby in the British Isles at the time, due to the fact that none of the four home nations could field a team good enough in that year to challenge a squad of grandmothers, that team has never been rated among the truly great touring parties.

There is also the trend in British sport—and not exclusively in British sport—to be over-critical, to gloss over genius and delve to find some weaknesses. We all spend longer bemoaning David Gower's supposed fragilities rather than sitting back and soaking up the glories of a sublime batsman. When Campese came back here in 1988 with Bob Dwyer's Wallabies, there were people wittering about his supposed weaknesses—the home coaches spoke about putting him under pressure.

The lineup. Second Test, Australia v
France, Paris. November 1993.

In one of the early matches on tour, Campese was on the left wing for Australia against the England B team, in a match played at Sale, south-west of Manchester. In the early stages, Dean Ryan, the giant no.8, came tearing around the fringes about 50 metres out, made a bee-line for Campese and in company with several large mates, drove hard at Campese, no doubt hoping to wipe out the Australian and leave him flat as a doormat, the perfect target for the following ruckers. The crowd cheered in delight as Ryan lowered his shoulder and hit Campese. The other forwards piled in.

To all those engrossed in the close-quarter melee it was something of a surprise to find that when all the players climbed back to their feet Campese was not at the bottom of the pile, winded and wounded. In fact, Campese was touching down for a try. As Ryan loomed, Campese had stolen in, stolen away the ball and simply sprinted off in glorious isolation down the left hand touchline while the England B attack continued without the ball. Campese scored two more tries in that match and moved into top gear along with the rest of the party when Michael Lynagh arrived late on tour to take charge.

At no point subsequent to that trip has Campese been regarded as less than a rugby god in the northern hemisphere. He has often said that he is more appreciated here than in Australia; it could well be true. The memories of the affection washing in waves from crowd after crowd is too vivid—Campese standing for almost an hour signing autographs at Leicester following a Barbarians match; Campese scoring against Wales at Cardiff in 1992, sprinting down the right wing in front of the North Stand to finally kill off a brave Welsh performance with a try—and yet the whole of that side of the ground swallowed its disappointment, rose and cheered Campese all the way back to the half-way line; Campese's two magical moments in the brilliant Australian World Cup semi-final win over New Zealand in Dublin in 1991—the first a snapping diagonal run across the face of the Kiwi defence for a try in the corner; the second, a breathtaking, blind pass behind his back to set up Tim Horan for another try in the same half of the same match, with Landsdowne Road cheering as if Campese had been as Irish as W.B. Yeats; and so many, many more.

Even the English have always been prepared to forgive. Campese's broadsides aimed at the front-on style of England rugby have been faithfully delivered to cause maximum stress. Yet apart from a few wounded ripostes from the likes of Brian Moore and Will Carling, the country in general has always been prepared to see Campese for precisely what he is—a gem of the game, a brilliant entertainer, and if he wants to be outspoken, then sit back and be entertained by that too.

My own sense of wonder derives only in part from the sheer attacking genius of the man, the fact that he could see plays long seconds before the opposition or even before his own team. For

(opposite at bottom) Young and fast, Australia v New Zealand, third Test, Auckland, 1982.
(below) It's all part of a superstar's job.

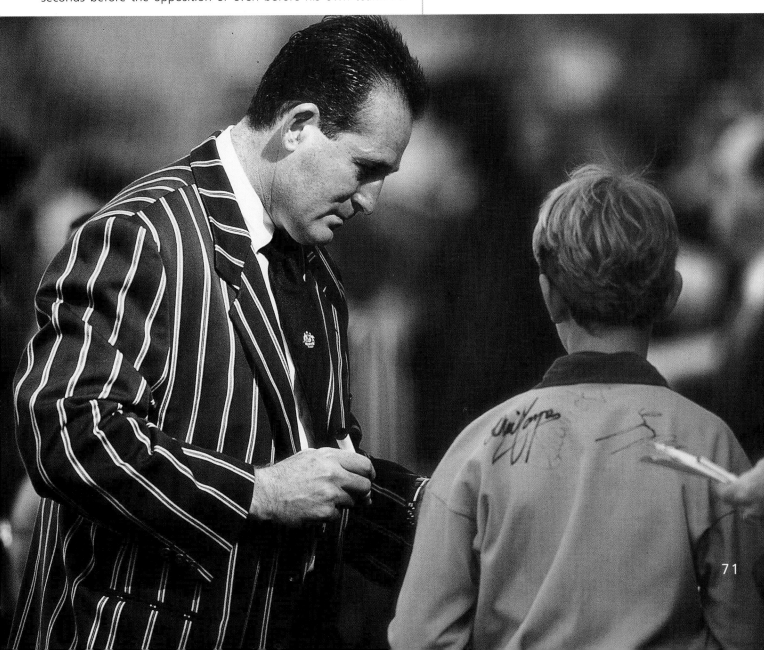

me, Campese was a complete footballing talent. Watching him from the end of the pitch during that 1988 tour you could see his superb defensive gifts, shadowing the inside man then tackling the outside man; at his best he is certainly one of the most extraordinary kickers of the dead ball the game has seen, and how priceless it has been for Australia to have a choice of two kickers to relieve the pressure, to keep the opposition guessing between Lynagh and Campese before they could try to harry the relieving kick.

In some quarters, Campese was thought of as some kind of showboating phenomenon, some frippery, someone who came on to keep the crowd keen with a few goose-steps before the real match recommenced. It was so much rubbish. As well as the matchless record for international tries, I always felt that Campese was the complete article, the complete rugby player. So he made a few defensive errors, some of them high-profile. How is a wing supposed to play more than ninety Tests, targeted for at least 300 high balls in his career and remain infallible? Campese is into credit by an enormous margin.

It was also a privilege to be present at one of his landmark occasions; indeed, to be present at what was conceivably the greatest week in the history of Australian rugby, greater even than the week in which they won the World Cup final in 1991.

It came in South Africa in 1992, when Dwyer, Nick Farr-Jones and the Australians made a short trip to South Africa to mark the end of the sporting isolation of that country. There was nothing ceremonial about the tour. Most Australians remembered the ridiculous banner carried around many venues of the 1991 World Cup. 'You aren't World Champs till you beat the Boks,' it said. It was a traumatic tour. A week before the Test match between South Africa and Australia at Cape Town had come the Die Stem incident, when months of slow progress in contacts between those old adversaries, the South African Rugby Board and the African National Congress, had been thrown sharply into reverse by the decision of the autocratic Louis Luyt of Transvaal to play the old white anthem before the Test against New Zealand. For several days, as the Wallabies waited with bags packed down in Port Elizabeth, it seemed as if the tour would be called off by the ANC, rightly incensed at attitudes within their own country.

Yet the statesmanlike stance of the Wallaby party, especially Farr-Jones and Joe French, ARU President, saved the trip, vastly impressed the ANC and vastly impressed those of us who always despaired at the ham-fisted approach to the South African question of most rugby administrators. Even Campese managed to bite his lip and maintain a diplomatic outer. In the Test match, inspired by a brilliant performance from Tim Horan, Australia wiped away the Springboks and laid to rest any suggestion that they did not deserve to call themselves the best rugby team in the

(above) This was the story of the night, Australia v Western Samoa, 1994. The home side scored seventy-three points at Sydney Football Stadium, a Test record for Australia.

world. And there came Campese, scuttling down the right wing near the end for his fiftieth Test try. Even as he touched down we turned to each other and said aloud that we could always claim to be present when the half-century was reached. If ever Australian rugby deserved to feel good about itself, Campese and everyone else, it was in South Africa in the spring of 1992.

In the British winter of 1996, Campese came with the New South Wales party. It was in some senses a low-key tour, fitted into the packed winter in midweek and, occasionally, in outposts of the country, as the New South Welshmen warmed up for their own southern hemisphere season ahead. Yet the old affections stirred one last time. The home teams all wanted to know right at the start of the tour if Campese would play against them. It made the world of difference to their marketing. If he was to front up, it meant a quickening of interest and anticipation. It meant that fathers would bring their youngsters along so that when they had youngsters of their own, they could claim, proudly, that they once saw play a singular, brilliant Australian called David Campese.

'He's an amazing athlete. He gets into a position where he is pivotal. You don't put restrictions on a guy like that. His greatest asset is his spontaneity.'

NSW coach Greg Smith in 1995

CHAMPION OF CHAMPIONS

by Phil Tresidder

Phil Tresidder has written about the game of rugby since 1946 and has seen all the great wing men of the postwar era. Here he compares David Campese with some of the other illustrious members of the group.

The smile of victory after
Randwick's 1992 grand final
win over Gordon.

They puff, they prance, they pirouette and, yes, often they pout, sometimes because they don't get the ball, other times because they do get it when it's not exactly convenient. They are the wingmen of rugby, princes of the game, darlings of the crowds. Only mothers could love those grizzly souls who crunch craniums in the bowels of the scrums, or for that matter stringbean lineout men who collect more mud than anybody else because they have elongated jerseys hanging outside their shorts. The flankers...well they've got a bit of dash and the halfbacks can be cocky entertainers. Some panache out there among the centres, maybe.

But the spotlight falls unfailingly on the wing three-quarters of rugby, just as it does the lead dancer in the ballet or the baton-swinging brass bandmaster. They are the speed kings. Given that golden inch of space they are off, spikes flashing, muscles taut and straining and the whole rugby world, it seems, giving chase. No wonder the fans jump to their feet in expectation.

It has been my good fortune to see all the great wingers of the post-war years. Better still, as a bonus and as an extremely young reporter along with Trevor Allan's 1947–48 Wallabies in the British Isles, I had a fleeting view of a pre-war personality. His name was C.B. (Cyril) Holmes and a shuffle through the record books will tell you he won both sprints on a Sydney Cricket Ground grass track at the 1938 British Empire Games. Well, he came out to do battle for Lancashire-Cheshire against the rampaging Wallabies and he laid the tourists low with two glorious tries.

The names of the great post-war wingers spill out. New Zealand, despite its forward fame, was richly endowed with Wally Argus, Grant Batty, Ron Jarden, Stu Wilson, John Kirwan and now the Man-Mountain himself, Jonah Lomu. France gave us Patrice Lagisquet, Fiji launched Joe Levula and there was Ken Jones of Wales and Tony O'Reilly of Ireland. Down Under we enjoyed a majestic succession of wing champions, starting with Charles Eastes, then Alan Morton, Ed Stapleton, Garth Jones, Ralph Garner and at this moment the matchless David Campese. Box office stuff, these fellows.

By and large most wing careers are short-circuited. The shuffling prop forward can hit the deck and clamber to his feet, shake himself and resume the battle with only pride ruffled. The wingman in full flight, by contrast, is a highly vulnerable and fragile target for high speed collision. Some of the greatest wingers seem to have come and vanished like exploding stars.

Argus toured with the first post-war All Blacks, strong and resourceful, then followed two lively rubber balls and masters of the touchdowns in Batty and Jarden. Jarden was not only a prolific try-scorer, but he converted them too. A point-scoring machine, quick-silver and a rare opportunist.

(above) The Man-Mountain Jonah Lomu, a fearful sight for chasers Jason Little (left) and Scott Bowen (right) as he strides away.
(right) French winger Patrice Lagisquet.

Stu Wilson took the knocks and was as durable an institution in All Black sides as was Kirwan, another fine finisher. New Zealand teams rarely ventured from their slogging-up-the-middle tactics, but once the ball was released to the backs for tactical kicks or strategic passes, Wilson and Kirwan knew where the tryline was.

Levula was perhaps the finest footballing athlete I ever saw and, like Lomu, a powerhouse winger blessed with astounding speed for his size. He was a catalyst for Fiji's sensational appearances on Australian grounds and the turf shuddered as the Wallaby fullback, Dick Tooth, fearlessly took him on with bootlace tackles. Tooth's mission was to halt a runaway express train.

Ken Jones, a track sprint champion, wore the scarlet of Wales with high distinction while O'Reilly had both speed and the ability to provide the unexpected. What else would you expect from an Irish wizard? He was a crowd idol before he hung up his sprigs and became a corporate giant. Peter Jackson was the best of the post-war English wingers, the most consummate side-stepper of them all, bringing the Wallabies of 1957–58 to grief at Twickenham with a zig-zagging try in injury time after the scores were deadlocked.

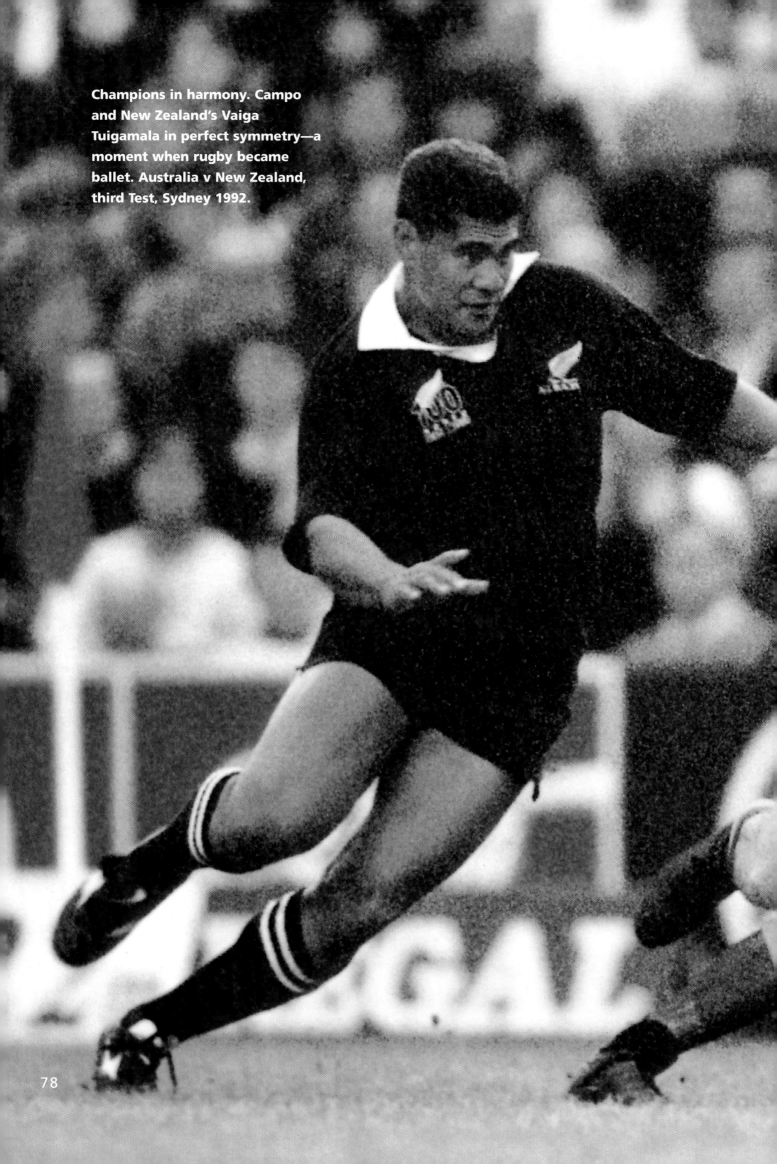

Champions in harmony. Campo and New Zealand's Vaiga Tuigamala in perfect symmetry—a moment when rugby became ballet. Australia v New Zealand, third Test, Sydney 1992.

British rugby knew it had a handful when the '47–48 Wallabies opened their tour against Cornwall–Devon and Charles Eastes from the Sydney club, Manly, with superb swerve and acceleration, raced in for successive tries. His tour was a triumph until cut tragically short in the match against Newport when he broke his arm. He never afterwards recaptured that winter's glory.

Alan Morton was our toughest winger, especially admired in New Zealand for his gutsy darting sorties. An asthmatic, the British winter of '57–58 brought him undone and he never approached his best. But at his best he was the fellow you wanted on your side when the Indians had the wagon train in their sights.

Garth Jones, a long-striding Queenslander, won everlasting fame when he cleared out at Newlands, Cape Town, to score the winning Wallaby try and inflict the first post-war defeat for the South African Springboks in 1953.

Sir Nicholas Shehadie, a long-serving prop and a member of that Wallaby team, rated Jones as the fastest winger he ever saw. Ed Stapleton proved a powerful customer in South Africa and he could turn a game with the unorthodox. He played with a smile on his face and the fans enjoyed this cheery big fellow from the St George club in Sydney. Ralph Garner burst on the scene one afternoon at the Sydney Showground where his brace of tries ignited Sydney University, winning the premiership against luckless Eastern Suburbs who had not lost a match all season. Garner was voted one of the five Players of the Year after a magnificent tour of New Zealand in 1949.

I look back on them all and wonder where David Campese stacks up in this exalted group. In truth, he doesn't resemble any of them, in technique, performance or personality. Good judges from the outset (especially New Zealanders) seemed wary about rating Campese, and I must confess I was one of them. Greatness is not an imprimatur to be bestowed lightly and among moments of inspiration there will inevitably be flawed execution and blemishes. The behind-the goal line Lions faux pas leaves a scar.

I watched one World Cup encounter with the Wallabies deep in the stygian gloom of a Welsh valley. The Aussies were slogging it out with Pacific rivals in the mud. Dull stuff for a winger. The cameramen, perhaps bored too, roamed their cameras across the field where Australian kingpin Campese was leaning nonchalantly against the goalpost. Clearly bored. It could have been a bush game at Wallabadah.

Campese is simply different from the other glamour wingmen of his day. Outspoken, too, whereas I cannot recall a single quote from the rest of the elite group. Campese took English rugby apart for its stultified tactics and failure to use gifted backs. The criticism did not sit too comfortably after England tumbled Australia out of the World Cup in South Africa, admittedly per medium of a dropped goal.

(opposite at top) **In a Randwick v Easts game, Campese offloads.** (opposite at bottom) **New Zealand's John Kirwan—one of the best.** (below) **'We are the champions.' Randwick, grand final winners (over Gordon), 1992.**

The Coogee rugby pitch, buffeted by breezes off the Pacific Ocean, has been Campese's personal patch. Week after week, fans of the Galloping Greens have been privileged to watch his wizardry for the Randwick club. Mostly, he seemed to toy with the opposition. But when the chips were down in the rugged 1992 grand final against Gordon at Waratah Park, with premiership honours hanging in the balance, he scored the clincher, a bullocking try in which he carried three hefty Highlanders over the line with him. A question mark has long hung over his defence and despite his size, Campese's physical play has never appeared his strongest point. Yet here was a confrontation that Lomu could not have bettered. I think that was the moment I knew he deserved the mantle of greatness.

Point-scoring achievements and Test match appearance records are falling to him like autumn leaves and will only help entrench his name in rugby's history books. He deserves his place there and, in truth, he will be remembered both as a character and champion when so many others will be forgotten. Since World War II I have seen them all. I wouldn't swap him for any of them.

'So easy. Campese.'

Oarsome Foursome rower Nick Green using a familiar catchphase after winning Olympic gold in Barcelona in 1992

THE GREATEST RUGBY PLAYER ON EARTH COMES FROM MARS

by Bryce Courtenay

Best-selling author and rugby aficionado Bryce Courtenay has been an ardent David Campese admirer ever since he left his home on the planet Mars.

New South Wales v Queensland, 1995.

want you to imagine that a Martian named Blott was watching the England-New Zealand semi-final game in the 1995 World Cup with the view of taking the game of rugby back to his home planet. He was a conscientious sort of bloke and made careful notes as the game progressed. The rules seemed simple enough to Blott, eight big men spend a lot of time in a huddle or standing in two rows, six smaller men stand in a line behind them and one other behind these. The ball comes out of the huddle and the object is to pass it to the man at the end of the line who must then run like hell to put the ball down across a given demarcation.

All this takes Blott about five minutes to understand so he settles down to watch for the finer points of the game. He soon discovers that getting the ball out to the man at the end of the line isn't quite as easy as it looks, there are heaps of mistakes on the way, players get knocked down, kick the ball away for no apparent reason, try to run on their own and even sometimes drop the ball at their feet.

After a while Blott concludes that sports lovers on Mars are unlikely to adopt what is plainly a scruffy rather stupid game played by a lot of clumsy, disinterested humans and he is just about to call it a day and summon up a spaceship when New Zealand get the ball and actually manage to pass it all the way across the

(above) Australia v USA, Sydney Cricket Ground, 1983. In only his fourth Test, Campese scored four tries, equalling the Australian record for the most tries in a Test. (right) A desperate moment, Australia v England, 1988 at Concord Oval, Sydney.

backline and into the hands of the biggest man on the field.

This man immediately sets off like an express train and runs straight down the sideline trampling dangerously on several players in white jerseys on the way. The crowd goes wild and the cheering lasts for several minutes.

That is, all but Blott, who fails to see the point and turns to a New Zealand supporter beside him, a man with his face painted in silver and black who is jumping up and down and crying and waving a flag with a fern motif and hugging and kissing everyone around him and generally making a bloody fool of himself.

'What's all the excitement about?' Blott asks, plainly bemused.

The Kiwi supporter stops weeping and hugging and looks at Blott aghast. 'Jonah Lomu! Jesus Christ, did you see what he just did to the bloody Poms!'

'All I saw was a very big man trample on a whole lot of much smaller men who were stupid enough to get in his way,' Blott replied.

'Damn right you did! Don't you know greatness when you see it? Where are you from, Mars or somewhere? Ferchrissake, you have just personally and with your own eyes witnessed the coming of a great winger and one of the greatest tries in history, man! Sex mighty points to En bloody Zed!'

Well, Blott knew an idiot when he saw one and didn't need the

silver fern on the flag or the war paint as verification. He politely excused himself and pressed the top button of his military-style tunic and was immediately sucked up into a passing spaceship and transported home.

Back on Mars he reported to the Minister for Sport.

'Well, Blott, how'd you go?' asked the Minister.

'Not good,' was the reply, 'It's all about brute force and big men. Martians are not very big and besides, are much too intelligent to play such a crude game.'

The Minister for Sport looked astonished. 'Are you sure you attended a *rugby* match, not a rugby league match, you know, *union*, the game they play in heaven?'

'Positive. The world championship, no less. The Whites versus the Blacks. England versus New Zealand who, I'm told on the best authority, look like ending up winning the World Cup. The general opinion is that they'll have to get food poisoning or something to stop them.'

The Minister scratched one of his heads. 'This doesn't compute. We've been sending Martian observers down to earth on a regular basis for some years now. Let me see, 1982 was the first such visit. Since then we've visited all the Earth countries who play the game and certainly we've never had a negative report like yours. May I ask, did you watch Australia play?'

'Well, no, they'd been eliminated.'

'How?'

'By a drop kick!'

'That's no way to talk about an international referee, Blott!'

The Minister for Sport spread his hands. 'Now I see it all. You didn't watch Australia, that's where you went wrong.' He went on to explain. 'You see, we've always monitored the game in a scientific way, one team as quality control, in our case, Australia, is chosen as the norm. We found that they are capable of the most inventive and stimulating game of all. Then over the years we've monitored the various Australian teams as they play against all the other teams, New Zealand, France, England, Ireland, Scotland, Wales, Argentina, Canada, even America and lately, South Africa, who, by the way, got their bottoms well and truly smacked by Australia in Cape Town in 1992 just for being arrogant pricks. We've been monitoring the game of rugby in this way since 1982 and, unlike you, Blott, your predecessors have been pretty bloody impressed. Did you see the C.V. Dossier before you left for Earth?'

'C.V. Dossier, sir?'

'Jesus, Blott!' You mean to say you didn't view the Campese Visual dossier? The thirteen years of painstaking research that went before you?'

'Well no, I've been rather busy lately.' Blott cleared his throat, 'But with the greatest respect, sir, I can sum the game up in two words, "Brute Force!"'

'You can't be serious, Blott?'

'Sir, no self-respecting Martian is going to get involved in this game from Hell. A game should have skill, subtlety and style, be inventive, surprising, exciting. I mean, there's not a smidgin of finesse, no brains, no invention! In the game I witnessed the All Blacks finally managed to pass the ball to a big gorilla at the end of the line, who, sniffing and grunting like a runaway locomotive, moved in a straight direction forward stamping dangerously on numerous smaller bodies who foolishly threw themselves down in his path! As for England, what a miserable lot they are, all they did was ruck, ruck, ruck then kick, kick, kick!'

The Minister for Sport pressed a button at his desk and a screen appeared on the wall opposite him. 'Sit down and don't say another word; you are about to see extracts from thirteen years of research taken from the C.V. Dossier.'

In the next half hour they watched as the young nineteen-year-old Campese scored his first try against the All Blacks in 1982 and then what followed on the screen was thirteen years of pure, joyous, Campese magic.

Blott was silent for a long time after the screen closed back to black. Then he leapt to his feet, waving his arms about. 'I

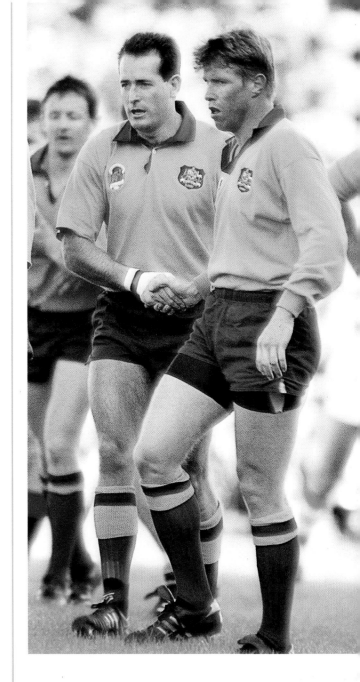

(above) **Campo the Canberra Raider—they wish! Glamour league side Canberra would have loved to have Campese in their ranks. This is as close as he got ... wearing their jumper.**

apologise, sir! I had no idea the game of rugby could be played like that. That an average-sized winger can do all those things without having to trample on anyone and without the use of brute force and ignorance. I mean, the sheer genius. The absolute beauty. The wonderful anticipation. The speed. The lightning passes. What reflexes! The way he reads the game. The handling skills. The side-step. The little punt ahead. The step off both feet. The raking touch finder. Did you see how he picks up a ball with one hand at full pelt? The goose-step, where did that come from? You have to see it to believe it. What an artist, magician, entertainer, joy, free spirit, buccaneer, this maestro of the unexpected! What dedication to fitness and character, all of it built on grinding hard work and self-belief! What a love of the game for the sheer fun of it, what wonderful motivation for Martian kids! Surely, David Ian Campese is one of the all-time great athletes!'

Blott turned to the Minister for Sport, tears running down his cheeks. 'Did you see the try he scored against the Barbarians at Cardiff Arms Park in 1988, sheer bloody out-of-this-world magic! Also, the diagonally run try against the All Blacks in the '91 World Cup, then later the blind flip pass over his shoulder to Horan. Is this the greatest rugby player in our time, or what!'

'Him and Mark Ella and Serge Blanco, but yes, Campo gets the number one spot,' the Minister agreed. 'Now listen to me, Blott, this is what I want you to do. God has challenged us to a series of Test matches and all the matches are to be played on Cloud Nine and, as you know, they've got every great player in the past to choose from. I want you to go back down to Earth and kidnap Campo, he needs eight more Tests to make his 100 and they're giving him a hard time at the moment. My guess is he shouldn't take a lot of persuasion to come, he's pretty tired of dickhead selectors and stumble-bum coaches. I want you to rotate him straight into the Martian Test team.'

Blott looked concerned, 'Kidnap him? I mean, after all, sir, he is an Earthling?'

The Minister for Sport sighed. 'You're pretty thick sometimes, Blott, are you sure you don't have a South African forward somewhere in your ancestry? If you'd only taken the trouble to read the bloody Dossier you'd know that Campo was kidnapped as a small child, taken from a nursery in the small town of Queanbeyan in Southern Mars. I mean, it doesn't take a lot of intelligence to see that anyone who plays rugby the way he does *has to be a bloody alien*. We want him back and we want him in time for the Test series against God! We may not be the best team in the universe but with Campo playing there'll be a little bit of sheer heaven on the wing.'

The Minister for Sport leaned back in his swivel chair and smiled, 'I can see the headline in the *Daily Firmament* now:

The greatest rugby player on earth comes from Mars!'

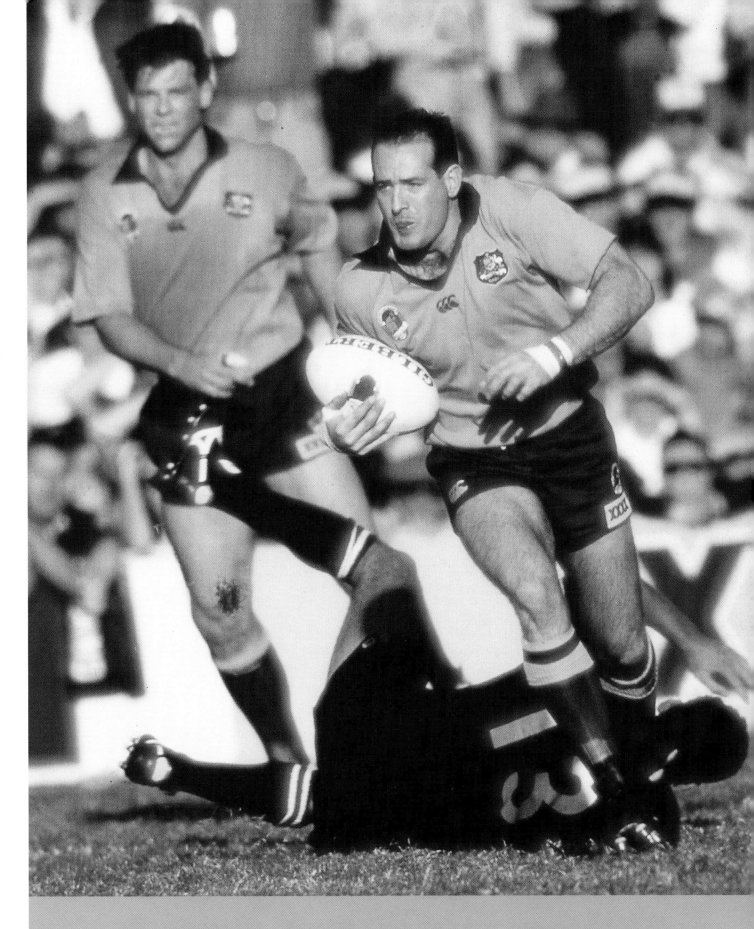

'Tell those lazy, "good-for-nothing" forwards to pull their fingers out and play properly. Tell them they are not heroes until they have won the World Cup— poofters!'

Good luck fax from Mark Ella on the eve of the 1991 World Cup final

LAST WORD

David Campese

92

Campo says g'day to a
namesake, the racehorse
So Easy Campese.

'You know, I don't ever want to be dropped from the team or injured so that I can't play. Deep down inside I want this to go on forever.'

PASTA
'Can-Peas-E'

A very quick and simple recipe, it's one of my favourites.

1 small onion, finely chopped
2 cloves of garlic, chopped
1 teaspoon of chopped dried chillies
2 tablespoons of extra virgin olive oil
1 can Edgell's peas
salt
freshly ground black pepper
500g pasta of your choice (I prefer Barilla's Penne Rigate)

1. Put the pasta on now as the sauce cooks in no time. Don't forget to cook the pasta in plenty of salted water.

2. Fry the onions, garlic and chillies in the oil until the onion is soft.

3. Add the drained peas and mix well.

4. Add salt and pepper to taste and simmer on low until the pasta is cooked.

5. Tip sauce into a serving bowl, quickly drain the pasta, add to the sauce, mix well and enjoy!

After New Zealand beat England in the semi-final of the 1995 World Cup I went back to the All Blacks dressing room to offer my congratulations. I was the only Australian there. I said 'Well done!' to Sean Fitzpatrick, the All Blacks captain. He thanked me and said, 'You know, Campo, the good thing about this game was that we really enjoyed playing.' It was refreshing to hear. This is what rugby should be all about—having a good time, enjoying yourself. If you don't enjoy playing, why play? This has always been my attitude, although I'm afraid enjoyment does not always rate as high in rugby as it should. I cannot remember when I last heard an Australian in the dressing room say how much he enjoyed the game he had just played.

An English journalist phoned me from London the other day to ask whether I thought the Five Nations teams were too concerned about winning and not concerned enough about playing the game. I said, 'Yes, obviously.' People pay at the turnstiles to be entertained. They come to see running rugby. So why kick the ball around for eighty minutes? Why bore everyone half to death by playing tactical rugby? The players don't do it for their own enjoyment. Quite the opposite. Anyone who has played the running game knows what an exciting, exhilarating, quite fantastic feeling it produces. So why would they want to play the kicking game instead? Wanting to win is the only possible explanation. Now we all accept that every team must try to win. I simply say winning isn't the be-all and end-all. You should try to win, but you

93

'I hope that by the time I finish I'll be so sick of the game that I won't want to go near it. I don't want to play Golden Oldies or anything like that. I just want to be remembered as a good rugby player.'

should try to win with a style of rugby that you enjoy playing and the spectators enjoy watching. My philosophy is: ignore the scoreboard and just play the best rugby you can. If your best is good enough to win, so much the better.

On the field I have always thought of myself as an entertainer. It is not a bad mental attitude to have because it guarantees you will at least try to play attractive rugby. Spectators who pay to see the match have a right to be entertained. A lot of Australians are irritated by the All Blacks' haka. I like it. It's entertaining for the public and so good for the game.

In her chapter, Tracey Holmes congratulates me for being honest in my public statements about the game. This is a nice change for me. Usually, I get criticised for shooting my mouth off. I have even heard it suggested that speaking out is somehow an ego trip for me. Some ego trip! Time after time, when I have spoken publicly about rugby, I have known beforehand that what I was saying would create problems for me. I knew I would suffer in one way or another by doing it. The reason I have done it—and keep doing it—is that I love rugby. I speak out for rugby, not for me.

When I do speak out, it is with the benefit of some experience. As I write this, I have been playing international rugby for fourteen years. Rules have changed. Styles of play have changed. I grew up in a game where people wanted to run the ball from everywhere. Admittedly, Australia was not as successful then as now, which means that now there is more pressure on us. Even so, we have generally become too negative in our approach. Because we have a reputation to protect, we take the safe options, the easy options. There have been Tests in recent years when we fell behind—and only then started running the ball. What we should do is run the ball right from the start. That is how you get the opposition on the back foot. Sure, if you're winning the match, you can afford to change tactics. But why leave it till the last ten minutes if you're behind?

When I made the Australian team as a nineteen-year-old I shut up and listened to the older players, hoping to learn as much as I could. Over the past four or five years, roughly since we won the World Cup, I have noticed a change in the younger players. There is money in the game now, the players are treated better and, I think, their egos have grown accordingly. I do know that the young guys are not as willing as we were to listen to older players

like myself. They think they know it all. That's a fact of life today, not only in rugby. Young people tend to be like that across the board.

Earlier in the book Stu Wilson tells the story of how I answered 'Stu who?' when a New Zealand TV reporter asked me in 1982 how I felt about marking him. The story is true, but Stu misunderstood why I said it. I didn't say it because I was cocky. I said it because I honestly did not know who Stu Wilson was. I was a nineteen-year-old boy from Queanbeyan. My background had been in rugby league, not rugby union. I hardly knew any rugby players outside those I played against in Australia. Even today my knowledge of players of the past is pretty thin. Phil Tresidder talks about some of the great wingers of the past in his chapter in this book. I have to be honest: many of the names mean nothing to me.

I should set the record straight on one other story involving Stu Wilson. At the end of the second Test of that same tour, I went up to Stu and said, 'You're not playing very well, Stu, are you?' What I meant was that here was a great All Black who had not been given an opportunity to show his ability. In other words, I was sympathising with him, one winger to another. The journalists did not present the story that way, I was written up as an arrogant nineteen-year-old who had tried to give the great All Black winger advice. That was the last thing I would have done. In those days, as I have mentioned before, I hardly said boo to anyone, even within my own team.

Stu raised another matter in his article that I feel strongly about. He said I was never into the physical, confrontational game that many others like to play. I play the game because I love playing

QUEANBEYAN RUGBY UNION FOOTBALL CLUB

The Mighty Whites

Queanbeyan's 17-year-old first grade fullback, David Campese, in action against Daramalan. During 1980 David represented ACT against NZ U21's and the ACTRU's President's XV against Australian Combined Services.

28th ANNUAL REPORT

for the year ended October 31, 1980.

NOTE: As this publication is going to press prior to October 31, 1980, the Statement of Income and Expenditure will be made available at the Annual General Meeting.

PAGE 11

(opposite at top) Memories of Italy: little David (right) with his sister Lisa, his grandfather and his brother Mario in northern Italy, 1996.
(opposite at bottom) With the school golf team, 1971. Campese is fourth from the left.
(above at top) Proud parents—with mum Joan and dad Antonio.
(above) Campese featured on the front cover of the Queanbeyan club's Annual Report in 1980, the year after his debut for the club.

it. I have never had any inclination to go out and try to belt some opponent or out-glare him. Glaring, in my opinion, is silly. I have marked some very physical players over the years, but I have never been drawn into any personal confrontation. Tuigamala was certainly a physical player, but he and I often exchanged smiles during a Test. That is how rugby should be played.

During the opening Super 12 New South Wales–Transvaal match in Sydney in 1995, I found that each time I kicked the ball out from a scrum or a ruck the Transvaal halfback Johan Roux came closer and closer to charging me down. Each time I kicked it out, I'd say to him, 'That was pretty close', and he would say, 'Yes—I'm getting closer.' We exchanged a laugh about it. Later, while we were watching the video of the match, some of the New South Wales players saw this and complained to me about it. They wondered why I was having a friendly exchange with an opponent on the field.

I was interested to see that Stu Wilson thinks I would have made a better fullback than a winger. It amazes me how many great players think I should play fullback while the coaches think I should play wing. My own view is that, yes, I would have liked to play fullback much more than I did. I do know that whenever I played fullback the opposition was not too keen to kick the ball to me because they knew if they kicked badly there was always a danger of a counter-attack. In 1994 I played about four matches in a row for Randwick on the wing without scoring a try. Then I played fullback in one match and scored three tries. The point is that a fullback can come in anywhere to get the ball, while the winger has to stay out there and wait for it to arrive. These days, a winger often has to wait a long, long time.

Stephen Jones refers in his chapter to the fact that I seem to have been better appreciated as a player in Europe than in Australia. If it is true, and I am sure it is, I have no doubt that the Australian media's attitude towards me is the reason. In Australia, the media wait for me to make a mistake. I know this to be true. I was watching the replay of a New South Wales match recently with a friend. When one of my kicks did not go out, the commentator made a point of saying it was a bad kick. My friend said at the time, 'How come when you do a bad kick they criticise you, but when anyone else does it, they don't say a word?' Whenever I miss a tackle, it seems to make the news. Against England in the 1995 World Cup, Damian Smith missed a tackle and England scored. If I had missed that tackle, the Australian media would have torn me to pieces. As it was, Damian's mistake hardly received a mention. I am not being critical of Damian here; after all, we have all missed tackles. I am simply making the point that I seem to be judged by different standards. I have been a tall poppy that the Australian media wanted to cut down.

Peter Jenkins has been watching me as a player for years, and

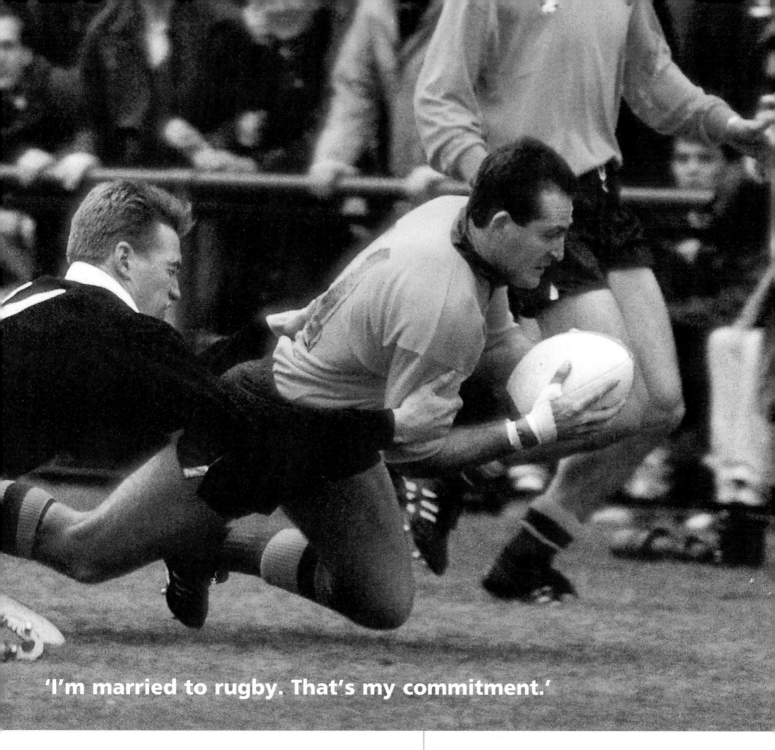

'I'm married to rugby. That's my commitment.'

he writes that Campese 'always trained to entertain and rarely misses a rehearsal.' I am happy to have this acknowledged. Whatever talent I may or may not have been born with, I have never believed that talent is enough, that you only have to turn up and it will work. I have always been fanatical about practising and training. Even when I was nineteen, I used to do extra training sessions during the week. I still do. I also tried to pick up as much as I could from other players. As a young player in 1981 or 1982 I remember seeing Michael O'Connor step twice before he beat his man. It seemed a smart idea, so I practised it, tried it, and it worked.

Referring to Mark Ella and myself, Gordon Bray writes in his chapter, 'My greatest regret in rugby is that these two kindred souls didn't play another five seasons or more together in Wallaby colours.' It is my greatest regret too. I think Mark Ella left the game too early. He thinks I have left my retirement too late. Nowadays, when I meet him and he asks how things are going, I will say,

'Gee, it's hard. It's getting harder and harder.' His reply is: 'So what are you playing for?' There is sense in what he says. Sometimes, on the field, I have thought to myself: 'What am I doing out here still?' The plain fact is I love rugby. I'll get out when I achieve what I want to achieve—or when I know I am not good enough to play.

Like Gordon Bray, I think Mark could have played for at least another five seasons. He was only twenty-four when he left, which seems to me a terrible waste of talent. I saw him playing in Italy in 1990. He had already let himself go and was overweight, but he was still a brilliant player. He really should have been in the winning World Cup team of 1991—which is no reflection at all on Michael Lynagh, who I consider a fantastic player. If Mark Ella had stayed fit, I honestly believe he could still be playing today. Rugby styles have changed since Ella played for Australia, but I have no doubt whatever that if the young Mark Ella came on the scene today, playing with the same skills that he played with then, he would still be a sensation.

I am pleased Alan Jones agreed to write a chapter in this book. I learned a lot of things from Alan during his few years as Australian coach. Probably the most important was to believe in yourself, to never doubt your own ability. Even over the past year, a difficult period in my rugby career, I have often spoken to him and he has been a great support. He is one who never lost faith in me as a player.

'It seems my whole life is in the fast lane. I'm always on a high, always hoping to achieve something.'

Alan Jones made sure we practised the basics, but he did not tell us how to play. What he did do was make us believe we were the best in the world. As a tactician, one of Jones' strong points was his ability to spot opposition weaknesses. Before we played Wales in 1984, he suggested we play the blinds. He had noticed the Welsh No. 8, Eddie Butler, had not played for three weeks and he had a hunch he would not be fit. So the first chance I got I went down the blind side and from that we scored under the posts.

At the time of writing, I have played under only two national coaches during my fourteen years in the Australian team, Alan Jones and Bob Dwyer. I noticed that Peter Jenkins mentioned Dwyer in passing, saying he was the only one to console me after my stuff-up behind the line in Sydney in 1989 that allowed the British Lions to score and win the match. This is true. I was sitting in the corner of the dressing room feeling shattered. Dwyer came up and said, 'Don't worry about it.' It wasn't much, but they were the only words of comfort I had that day, and I have not forgotten them.

As I admitted earlier, not being too strong on rugby history, I am not too familiar with quite a few of the wingers Phil Tresidder mentions in his interesting chapter. I do know something about those wingers I have played with or against, however. I particularly admired three of them. One was my old Australian teammate

(opposite) David Campese and the man who is heir apparent to the mantle of the world s greatest rugby winger, Jonah Lomu.
(above) The battle over ... time for a beer, a yarn, a smile. Campese with John Kirwan after Australia v New Zealand third Test, 1992.
(below) In full stride against South Africa, Sydney, 1993.

(below) Campo the golfer—His favourite recreation.
(at bottom) At Campo's Sport and Leisure Store, St Ives, Sydney.
(right) With Australian rules football superstar Gary Ablett.

'I know people will think I'm stupid but I don't think rugby should ever be played for money. Money helps, but it's not life. So what's it all for? It's for friendship and loyalty, and all the fun you can have playing and, preferably, winning. And those things are better than money any day.'

Brendan Moon. He was well established in the Australian team when I arrived, and he was a good player to watch and learn from. He was not the world's most explosive player, but when he did something he did it well. He also appeared to do things easily, the mark of a well-balanced player. John Kirwan was another winger I really admired. He was a strong, aggressive player, and he got the better of me quite a few times. With the ball in his hands JK was very determined. He had a job to do and it did not matter who was in front of him. I was sorry his rugby career ended the way it did. It still amazes me how selectors can drop a winger when the winger has been given no opportunity to perform. The third of my favourite wingers is Serge Blanco. He *was* a great player, whether he played as fullback or winger. He was the most skillful winger I have played against and you had to watch him all the time.

Bill McLaren, who wrote a chapter for this book, is one of those commentators who would rather say something good about you than bad, and there aren't many of them. It is simply not in Bill's nature to bag players. I also respect him for his knowledge of the game. He is right to emphasise the importance of unpredictability. On the field, my number one objective is to keep the player marking me in two minds, not knowing if I will go this way or that, whether I will run, step, or swerve, or kick.

Mark Ella also picks up on this point. Nobody has influenced me more as a player than Mark. When I first made the Australian team in 1982 he was already my hero. I learned to think and play like Ella on the field, which basically meant thinking and playing smart. The essence of Ella's game was to confuse your opponent, to make him wonder what you intended to do next. Not everyone plays like this. As Mark points out, Jonah Lomu does not bother trying to confuse anyone. His opponents always know what Jonah is going to do, but they are often unable to stop him doing it. Jonah has the size, speed and power to run over people. You know that when he gets the ball he will not try to kick. He will simply try to run over you or around you, whichever is the more direct. Lomu's is obviously a different talent from mine, but it is a great talent. In its first year, 1996, the Super 12 tournament was a bigger success than probably anyone guessed it would be. The fact it was a hit with the rugby public was obvious from the size of the crowds. The players enjoyed it, too, although I do think some found it difficult to perform well in such a high class of rugby, week after week, in one city after another. In many ways, it was like playing eleven Test matches, because the standard of the play was consistently very high. In the case of my own team, New South Wales, I am sure the younger players learned a lot from the experience. In particular they learned that you really have to work hard to maintain a high standard of play in this type of competition—that if you turn in one good performance you cannot then afford to coast through the next few matches. So the Super 12 was good for the spectators, it was good for the players and I am certain it was good for the game, because the exposure it received during the competition did a lot to lift rugby's profile.

Rugby has been good to me. I came from a town of 24,000 people. I didn't finish school and I have certainly never thought of myself as an intellectual. If it had not been for rugby, I would probably still be at the sawmill in Queanbeyan where I started work when I left school. On the rugby field, though, I know what I can do. I have always known I could do things nobody else could do, and when I get the ball I try to do something different. I'm prepared to take the chance. I'm willing to try to do a thing that may look impossible. If it doesn't work, well, so be it. But you have to keep on trying.

'I suppose it's an honour, but all it really is is the letter C after your name.'

David Campese on leading the NSW Waratahs for only the second time in the opening tour match against Bristol in January 1996. Teammates always chuckle at Campese captaining a team because it means he cannot indulge his superstition of running onto the field last

STATISTICS

(as at 22 June 1996)

Legend

ⓕ *- fullback*
pen - penalty
conv - conversion
* - World Cup Match

David Ian Campese

Date of birth: 21st October, 1962
Height: 180cm
Weight: 90kg
Position: wing/full–back
Representative honours: Australian Capital Territory Under 21s,
Australian Capital Territory, Australian Under 21s, New South Wales,
Barbarians, Australian Sevens, Australia
Club honours: Queanbeyan Whites, Randwick, Petrarca,
Mediolanum Amatori
Test debut: against New Zealand at Lancaster Park, Christchurch,
14 August, 1982

Australia

Test	Date	Versus	Result for Australia	Score	Venue	Campese
1	14 Aug 82	New Zealand	Lost	16–23	Christchurch	1 try
2	28 Aug 82	New Zealand	Won	19–16	Wellington	1 try
3	11 Sept 82	New Zealand	Lost	18–33	Auckland	–
4	9 July 83	USA	Won	49–3	Sydney	4 tries, 1 conv
5	31 July 83	Argentina	Lost	3–18	Brisbane	1 pen
6	7 Aug 83	Argentina	Won	29–13	Sydney	1 try, 3 conv, 1 pen ⨍
7	20 Aug 83	New Zealand	Lost	8–18	Sydney	– ⨍
8	22 Oct 83	Italy	Won	29–7	Padua	3 conv, 1 pen
9	13 Nov 83	France	Draw	15–15	Clermont Ferrand	1 conv, 1 pen
10	19 Nov 83	France	Lost	6–15	Paris	1 pen
11	9 June 84	Fiji	Won	16–3	Suva	1 try
12	21 July 84	New Zealand	Won	16–9	Sydney	–
13	4 Aug 84	New Zealand	Lost	15–19	Brisbane	1 pen
14	18 Aug 84	New Zealand	Lost	24–25	Sydney	1 try, 1 pen
15	3 Nov 84	England	Won	19–3	Twickenham	–
16	10 Nov 84	Ireland	Won	16–9	Dublin	–
17	24 Nov 84	Wales	Won	28–9	Cardiff	–
18	8 Dec 84	Scotland	Won	37–12	Murrayfield	2 tries
19	10 Aug 85	Fiji	Won	52–28	Brisbane	1 drop goal
20	17 Aug 85	Fiji	Won	31–9	Sydney	2 tries
21	1 June 86	Italy	Won	39–18	Brisbane	2 tries

Test	Date	Versus	Result for Australia	Score	Venue	Campese
22	21 June 86	France	Won	27–14	Sydney	1 try ⓕ
23	6 July 86	Argentina	Won	39–19	Brisbane	1 try ⓕ
24	12 July 86	Argentina	Won	26–0	Sydney	2 tries ⓕ
25	9 Aug 86	New Zealand	Won	13–12	Wellington	1 try ⓕ
26	23 Aug 86	New Zealand	Lost	12–13	Dunedin	– ⓕ
27	6 Sept 86	New Zealand	Won	22–9	Auckland	1 try
28	23 May 87	England*	Won	19–6	Sydney	1 try
29	31 May 87	USA*	Won	47–12	Brisbane	1 try
30	3 June 87	Japan*	Won	42–23	Sydney	1 try ⓕ
31	7 June 87	Ireland*	Won	33–15	Sydney	– ⓕ
32	13 June 87	France*	Lost	24–30	Sydney	1 try ⓕ **World record for Test tries**
33	18 June 87	Wales*	Lost	21–22	Rotorua	–
34	25 July 87	New Zealand	Lost	16–30	Sydney	–
35	29 May 88	England	Won	22–16	Brisbane	–
36	12 June 88	England	Won	28–8	Sydney	1 try
37	3 July 88	New Zealand	Lost	7–32	Sydney	–
38	16 July 88	New Zealand	Draw	19–19	Brisbane	–
39	30 July 88	New Zealand	Won	30–9	Sydney	–
40	5 Nov 88	England	Lost	19–28	London	1 try
41	19 Nov 88	Scotland	Won	32–13	Murrayfield	2 tries
42	3 Dec 88	Italy	Won	55–6	Rome	3 tries
43	1 July 89	British Lions	Won	30–12	Sydney	–
44	8 July 89	British Lions	Lost	12–19	Brisbane	–
45	15 July 89	British Lions	Lost	18–19	Sydney	–
46	5 Aug 89	New Zealand	Lost	12–24	Auckland	1 try
47	4 Nov 89	France	Won	32–15	Strasbourg	1 try
48	11 Nov 89	France	Lost	19–25	Lille	– ⓕ
49	24 June 90	France	Won	48–31	Brisbane	1 try ⓕ
50	30 June 90	France	Lost	19–28	Sydney	50th Test, 1 try ⓕ
51	8 July 90	USA	Won	67–9	Brisbane	1 try, 1 drop goal
52	21 July 90	New Zealand	Lost	6–21	Christchurch	– ⓕ
53	4 Aug 90	New Zealand	Lost	17–27	Auckland	–
54	18 Aug 90	New Zealand	Won	21–9	Wellington	–
55	21 July 91	Wales	Won	63–6	Brisbane	1 try
56	27 July 91	England	Won	40–15	Sydney	2 tries
57	10 Aug 91	New Zealand	Won	21–12	Sydney	–
58	24 Aug 91	New Zealand	Lost	3–6	Auckland	–
59	4 Oct 91	Argentina*	Won	32–19	Llanelli	2 tries
60	9 Oct 91	Western Samoa*	Won	9–3	Pontypool	**Australian record for Test appearances**
61	12 Oct 91	Wales*	Won	38–4	Cardiff	1 try
62	20 Oct 91	Ireland*	Won	19–18	Dublin	2 tries
63	27 Oct 91	New Zealand*	Won	16–6	Dublin	1 try

Test	Date	Versus	Result for Australia	Score	Venue	Campese
64	2 Nov 91	England*	Won	12–6	Twickenham	**100th game for Aust.**
65	13 June 92	Scotland	Won	27–12	Sydney	2 tries
66	21 June 92	Scotland	Won	37–13	Brisbane	–
67	4 July 92	New Zealand	Won	16–15	Sydney	1 try
68	19 July 92	New Zealand	Won	19–17	Brisbane	–
69	25 July 92	New Zealand	Lost	23–26	Sydney	–
70	22 Aug 92	South Africa	Won	26–3	Cape Town	1 try **(50th Test try)**
71	31 Oct 92	Ireland	Won	42–17	Dublin	1 try
72	21 Nov 92	Wales	Won	23–6	Cardiff	1 try
73	4 July 93	Tonga	Won	52–14	Brisbane	2 tries
74	17 July 93	New Zealand	Lost	25–10	Dunedin	–
75	31 July 93	South Africa	Lost	12–19	Sydney	–
76	14 Aug 93	South Africa	Won	28–20	Brisbane	–
77	21 Aug 93	South Africa	Won	19–12	Sydney	–
78	9 Oct 93	Canada	Won	43–16	Edmonton	3 tries
79	30 Oct 93	France	Lost	13–16	Bordeaux	–
80	6 Nov 93	France	Won	24–3	Paris	–
81	5 June 94	Ireland	Won	33–13	Brisbane	1 try
82	11 June 94	Ireland	Won	32–18	Sydney	–
83	18 June 94	Italy	Won	23–20	Brisbane	–
84	25 June 94	Italy	Won	20–7	Melbourne	1 try
85	8 Aug 94	Western Samoa	Won	73–3	Sydney	1 try
86	17 Aug 94	New Zealand	Won	20–16	Sydney	–
87	30 Apr 95	Argentina	Won	53–7	Brisbane	1 try
88	6 May 95	Argentina	Won	30–13	Sydney	2 tries
89	25 May 95	South Africa*	Lost	18–27	Cape Town	–
90	31 May 95	Canada*	Won	27–11	Port Elizabeth	–
91	10 June 95	England*	Lost	22–25	Cape Town	–
92	29 July 95	New Zealand	Lost	23–34	Sydney	*ran on as replacement*
93	8 June 96	Wales	Won	56-25	Brisbane	-
94	22 June 96	Wales	Won	42-3	Sydney	

Summary of Test matches v all Nations

Versus	Played	Won	Lost	Drawn	Tries	Conv	Pen	Goal	Points
Argentina	7	6	1	–	9	3	2	–	51
British Lions	3	1	2	–	–	–	–	–	–
Canada	2	2	–	–	3	–	–	–	15
England	8	6	2	–	5	–	–	–	20
Fiji	3	3	–	–	3	–	–	1	15
France	10	4	5	1	5	1	2	–	28
Ireland	6	6	–	–	4	–	–	–	18
Italy	5	5	–	–	6	3	1	–	34
Japan	1	1	–	–	1	–	–	–	4
New Zealand	27	11	15	1	8	–	2	–	39
Scotland	4	4	–	–	6	–	–	–	24
South Africa	5	3	2	–	1	–	–	–	5
Tonga	1	1	–	–	2	–	–	–	10
USA	3	3	–	–	6	1	–	1	29
Wales	7	7	1	–	3	–	–	–	13
Western Samoa	2	2	–	–	1	–	–	–	5
Total	**94**	**65**	**28**	**2**	**63**	**8**	**7**	**2**	**310**

Note: Since 1992 tries have been awarded 5 points

New South Wales

Match	Date	Versus	Result for NSW	Score	Venue	Campese
1	11 April 87	Canterbury	Won	25–24	Christchurch	1 try
2	19 April 87	Auckland	Lost	18–19	Sydney	1 try
3	25 April 87	Fiji	Won	23–20	Suva	2 tries
4	3 May 87	Wellington	Won	40–15	Sydney	2 tries
5	10 May 87	Queensland	Lost	6–17	Brisbane	–
6	19 June 88	Queensland	Won	27–18	Brisbane	1 try
7	23 June 88	New Zealand	Lost	6–42	Sydney	–
8	24 June 89	British Lions	Lost	21–23	Sydney	–
9	23 June 91	Queensland	Won	21–12	Sydney	–
10	7 July 91	England	Won	21–19	Sydney	–
11	14 July 91	Wales	Won	71–8	Sydney	5 tries
12	6 June 93	Queensland	Lost	17–29	Sydney	–
13	13 June 93	Queensland	Lost	15–37	Brisbane	–
14	24 July 93	South Africa	Won	29–28	Sydney	–
15	29 Mar 94	Wanganui	Won	81–17	Wanganui	–
16	3 April 94	Waikato	Won	43–16	Hamilton	–
17	10 April 94	Western Samoa	Won	25–23	Sydney	drop goal
18	20 April 94	ACT	Won	45–14	Sydney	1 try
19	1 May 94	Auckland	Won	22–19	Sydney	1 try
20	22 May 94	Ireland	Won	55–18	Sydney	2 tries
21	9 July 94	Queensland	Lost	20–22	Brisbane	drop goal
22	17 July 94	Queensland	Won	38–8	Sydney	–
23	22 Feb 95	Western Australia	Won	65–10	Perth	–
24	25 Feb 95	Zimbabwe	Won	76–10	Harare	–
25	4 Mar 95	Transvaal	Lost	18–21	Johannesburg	–
26	10 Mar 95	Otago	Won	31–16	Sydney	–
27	25 Mar 95	Western Province	Won	23–21	Sydney	–
28	3 July 95	Otago	Won	44–29	Dunedin	2 tries
29	9 July 95	Queensland	Won	33–21	Sydney	–
30	16 July 95	Queensland	Won	30–23	Brisbane	–
31	22 Jan 96	Bristol	Won	34–23	Bristol	–
32	31 Jan 96	England A	Lost	22–24	Leicester	–
33	2 Feb 96	Leinster	Won	33–19	Dublin	–
34	6 Feb 96	Ulster	Won	40–33	Belfast	–
35	1 Mar 96	Transvaal	Won	32-11	Sydney	–
36	9 Mar 96	Western Province	Won	30-22	Cape Town	–
37	16 Mar 96	Northern Transvaal	Lost	29–32	Pretoria	–
38	24 Mar 96	ACT	Won	44–6	Sydney	1 try
39	29 Mar 96	Canterbury	Lost	16-21	Christchurch	–
40	2 April 96	Natal	Lost	6-34	Sydney	–

Match	Date	Versus	Result for NSW	Score	Venue	Campese
41	14 April 96	Queensland	Lost	6-34	Sydney	-
42	21 April 96	Otago	Won	29-25	Sydney	1 try
43	28 April 96	Waikato	Lost	17-39	Hamilton	-
44	1 May 96	Auckland	Lost	44-56	Auckland	1 try
45	10 May 96	Wellington	Won	52-25	Sydney	1 try
46	1 June 96	Queensland	Won	29-25	Sydney	-

Most appearances in major internationals

(as at 22 June 1996)

Player		Games	Test Career
1	Philippe Sella, France	111	1982–95
2	**David Campese, Australia**	**94**	**1982–96**
3	Serge Blanco, France	93	1980–91
4	Rory Underwood, England	91**	1984–96
5	Mike Gibson, Ireland	81**	1964–79
6	Willie-John McBride, Ireland	80**	1962–75
7	Rob Andrew, England	75**	1985–95
8	Sean Fitzpatrick, New Zealand	75	1986–95
9	Michael Lynagh, Australia	72	1984–95
10	Roland Bertranne, France	69	1971–81
11	Brian Moore, England	69	1987–95

** *includes appearances for British Isles*

Most tries in major internationals

	Player	Tries	Games	Career
1	**David Campese, Australia**	**63**	**94**	**1982–96**
2	Rory Underwood, England	50	91	1984–96
3	Serge Blanco, France	38	93	1980–91
4	John Kirwan, New Zealand	35	63	1984–94
5	Philippe Sella, France	30	111	1982–95
6	Philippe Saint-Andre, France	29	59	1990–96
7	Ieuan Evans, Wales	28	67	1987–96
8	Ian Smith, Scotland	24	34	1924–33
9	Christian Darrouy	23	40	1957–67
10	Gerald Davies, Wales	23	51	1966–78

Source: Rothmans Rugby Union Yearbook 1995/96

Leading Australian Test players

	Player	Games	Test Career
1	**David Campese, NSW**	**94**	**1982–95**
2	Michael Lynagh, Qld	72	1984–95
3	Nick Farr–Jones, NSW	63	1984–93
4	Simon Poidevin, NSW	59	1980–91
5	Phil Kearns, NSW	49	1989–95
6	Ewen McKenzie, NSW	47	1990–96
7	Tim Gavin, NSW	44	1988–95
8	Peter Johnson, NSW	42	1959–71
9	Tom Lawton, Qld	41	1983–89
10	Tony Daly, NSW	41	1989–95
11	Tony Miller, NSW	41	1952–67

Team of the Decade

To mark the end of a decade of international rugby in 1989, the bible of world rugby—the Rothmans Rugby Union Yearbook—chose their Team of the Decade. The panel agreed that one selection was straightforward, that of David Campese on the left wing.

The team was chosen by panel from the cream of the world's leading players: Gareth Edwards, former French captain Jean-Pierre Rives, former Scottish fly-half Ian Robertson, and David Kirk, who led New Zealand to their World Cup triumph in 1991. The criterion for selection was that the players must have played international rugby in the 1980s and each was judged on his ability at his peak.

The full team was

FULL-BACK
Serge Blanco (France)

RIGHT WING
John Kirwan (New Zealand)

CENTRE
Danie Gerber (South Africa)

CENTRE
Philippe Sella (France)

LEFT WING
David Campese (Australia)

FLY-HALF
Hugo Porta (Argentina)

SCRUM HALF
Dave Loveridge (New Zealand)

PROP
Robert Paparemborde (France)

HOOKER
Colin Deans (Scotland)

PROP
Graham Price (Wales)

LOCK
Steve Cutler (Australia)

LOCK
Andy Haden (New Zealand)

FLANKER
Michael Jones (New Zealand)

NO 8
Morne du Plessis (South Africa)

FLANKER
Graham Mourie (New Zealand)
(captain)

If

If you can keep your head
    when all about you
Are losing theirs
    and blaming it on you,
If you can trust yourself
    when all men doubt you,
But make allowance
    for their doubting too;
If you can wait and
    not be tired by waiting,
Or being lied about,
    don't deal in lies,
Or being hated,
    don't give way to hating,
And yet don't look too good,
    not talk too wise;

If you can dream—and not
    make dreams your master;
If you can think—and not
    make thoughts your aim;
If you can meet with
    Triumph and Disaster
And treat those two
    Imposters just the same.

If you can make one heap
    of all your winnings
And risk it on one turn
of pitch-and-toss;
And lose, and start again
    at your beginnings,
And never breathe a word
    about your loss.

If you can talk with crowds
    and keep your virtue
Or walk with Kings—not lose
    the common touch,
If neither foes nor loving
friends
    can hurt you,
If all men count with you,
    but none too much;

If you can fill the
    unforgiving minute
With sixty seconds' worth
    of distance run,
Yours is the Earth and
    everything that's in it,
And—which is more
    —you'll be a Man, my son!

Rudyard Kipling

PHOTO ACKNOWLEDGEMENTS

Front end paper: Action photographics; page 3: Action Photographics; page 6: Action Photographics; page 7: C Golding/Fairfax Photo Library; page 8-9: Australian Picture Library/Allsport/Bruty; page 10: Andrew Dawson/Sportshot; page 11: Action Photographics; page 13: Craig Golding/Fairfax Photo Library Photo Library; Australian Picture Library/Allsport; page 16: Action Photographics/Fotopacific; Action Photographics/Fotopacific; page 17: Live Action; Australian Picture Library; News Ltd; page 18-19: Action Photographics/Colorsport; page 20: Action Photographics; page 21: Action Photographics; page 23: Action Photographics; page 24: Action Photographics; page 25: Action Photographics; page 26: Action Photographics; page 27: Action Photographics/Colorsport; page 28: Australian Picture Library/Olympia; page 29: Andrew Taylor/Fairfax Photo Library; page 31: Action Photographics; page 32: Sport. The Library; page 33: Shaun Botterill/Allsport; page 34: Mirror Australian Telegraph Publications; Action Photographics; page 35: Action Photographics; page 36: Australian Picture Library/Allsport; page 36-37: David Rogers/Allsport; page 38: Action Photographics; page 39: Barry McKinnon/Mirror Australian Telegraph Publications; page 41: Action Photographics; page 44: News Ltd; page 44-45: Verdat Acikalin/Live Action; page 45: Australian Picture Library/Allsport; page 46: Action Photographics; page 47: AP Photo; page 49: AAP; page 50: Russell Cheyne/Australian Picture Library/Allsport; page 51: Mike Powell/Australian Picture Library/Allsport; Fairfax Photo Library; page 52: Action Photographics; page 53: Mirror Australian Telegraph Publications/Action Photographics/Fotopacific; page 54: Action Photographics/Colorsport; Action Photographics; page 55: Sportsphoto; page 57: Live Action; page 58: Mirror Australian Telegraph Publications; page 59: Australian Picture Library/Vann/Yann Guichaoua; page 60: Action Photographics/Colorsport; page 61: Action Photographics; Allsport; page 62: Action Photographics; Simon Alekna/Fairfax Photo Library; page 63: Action Photographics; Vedat Acikalin; Live Action; page 64: Action Photographicspage 65: Action Photographics/Cox; page 66: Action Photographics; page 67: Action Photographics/Colorsport; page 68: Action Photographics; page 70: Allsport; Action Photographics; page 71: Australian Picture Library/J Carnemolla; page 72-73: Dallas Kilponen/Fairfax Photo Library; page 75: Australian Picture Library/Bruce Palme; page 76: David Cannon/Allsport; page 78-79: Australian Picture Library/Bruce Palme; page 80: Andrew Taylor/Fairfax Photo Library; Action Photographics; page 81: Allsport; page 83: Australian Picture Library/Joe Mann; page 84: Action Photographics; page 85: Brendan Read/Fairfax Photo Library; Mirror Australian Telegraph Publications; page 86: Sport. The Library; Australian Picture Library/Joe Mann; page 87: Russell Cheyne/Allsport; page 88: Peter Morris/Fairfax Photo Library; page 89: Action Photographics; page 91: Action Photographics; page 95: Mirror Australian Telegraph Publications; page 97: Action Photographics/ Fotopacific; page 98: Chris Kapetanellis/Live Action; page 99: Allsport; page 100: Australian Picture Library/Charbaux; Action Photographics; page 100-101: Action Photographics; page 101: Russell Cheyne/Allsport; page 103: Action Photographics; page 104: David Gadd/Sportsphoto Agency; page 107: Action Photographics; page 108: Allsport; page 111: Fairfax Photo Library; page 112: Australian Picture Library/Charbaux. Back endpaper: Simon Bruty/Allsport